EVERYMAN'S LIBRARY
POCKET POETS

HARDY

POEMS

EVERYMAN'S LIBRARY
POCKET POETS

This selection by Peter Washington first published in
Everyman's Library, 1995
© David Campbell Publishers Ltd., 1995

ISBN 1-85715-717-6

A CIP catalogue record for this book is available from the British Library

Published by David Campbell Publishers Ltd.,
79 Berwick Street, London W1V 3PF

Distributed by Random House (UK) Ltd.,
20 Vauxhall Bridge Road, London SW1V 2SA

Typography by Peter B. Willberg

Typeset by MS Filmsetting Ltd., Frome, Somerset

Printed and bound in Germany by
Mohndruck Graphische Betriebe GmbH, Gütersloh

CONTENTS

MB

*Starred part-titles are the Editor's.

THOMAS HARDY

POEMS

ANY LITTLE OLD SONG

Any little old song
   Will do for me,
Tell it of joys gone long,
   Or joys to be,
Or friendly faces best
   Loved to see.

Newest themes I want not
   On subtle strings,
And for thrillings pant not
   That new song brings:
I only need the homeliest
   Of heartstirrings.

HEREDITY

HEREDITY

I am the family face;
Flesh perishes, I live on,
Projecting trait and trace
Through time to times anon,
And leaping from place to place
Over oblivion.

The years-heired feature that can
In curve and voice and eye
Despise the human span
Of durance – that is I;
The eternal thing in man,
That heeds no call to die.

THE ROMAN ROAD

The Roman Road runs straight and bare
As the pale parting-line in hair
Across the heath. And thoughtful men
Contrast its days of Now and Then,
And delve, and measure, and compare;

Visioning on the vacant air
Helmed legionaries, who proudly rear
The Eagle, as they pace again
                        The Roman Road.

But no tall brass-helmed legionnaire
Haunts it for me. Uprises there
A mother's form upon my ken,
Guiding my infant steps, as when
We walked that ancient thoroughfare,
                        The Roman Road.

TRANSFORMATIONS

Portion of this yew
Is a man my grandsire knew,
Bosomed here at its foot:
This branch may be his wife,
A ruddy human life
Now turned to a green shoot.

These grasses must be made
Of her who often prayed,
Last century, for repose;
And the fair girl long ago
Whom I often tried to know
May be entering this rose.

So, they are not underground,
But as nerves and veins abound
In the growths of upper air,
And they feel the sun and rain,
And the energy again
That made them what they were!

LOGS ON THE HEARTH

A MEMORY OF A SISTER

The fire advances along the log
    Of the tree we felled,
Which bloomed and bore striped apples by the peck
    Till its last hour of bearing knelled.

The fork that first my hand would reach
    And then my foot
In climbings upward inch by inch, lies now
    Sawn, sapless, darkening with soot.

Where the bark chars is where, one year,
    It was pruned, and bled –
Then overgrew the wound. But now, at last,
    Its growings all have stagnated.

My fellow-climber rises dim
    From her chilly grave –
Just as she was, her foot near mine on the bending
    limb,
    Laughing, her young brown hand awave.

DECEMBER 1915

ON ONE WHO LIVED AND
DIED WHERE HE WAS BORN

When a night in November
   Blew forth its bleared airs
An infant descended
   His birth–chamber stairs
   For the very first time,
   At the still, midnight chime;
All unapprehended
   His mission, his aim. –
Thus, first, one November,
An infant descended
     The stairs.

On a night in November
   Of weariful cares,
A frail aged figure
   Ascended those stairs
   For the very last time:
   All gone his life's prime,
All vanished his vigour,
   And fine, forceful frame:
Thus, last, one November
Ascended that figure
     Upstairs.

On those nights in November –
    Apart eighty years –
The babe and the bent one
    Who traversed those stairs
    From the early first time
    To the last feeble climb –
That fresh and that spent one –
    Were even the same:
Yea, who passed in November
As infant, as bent one,
      Those stairs.

Wise child of November!
    From birth to blanched hairs
Descending, ascending,
    Wealth-wantless, those stairs;
    Who saw quick in time
    As a vain pantomime
Life's tending, its ending,
    The worth of its fame.
Wise child of November,
Descending, ascending
      Those stairs!

WESSEX HEIGHTS
(1896)

There are some heights in Wessex,
    shaped as if by a kindly hand
For thinking, dreaming, dying on,
    and at crises when I stand,
Say, on Ingpen Beacon eastward,
    or on Wylls-Neck westwardly,
I seem where I was before my birth,
    and after death may be.

In the lowlands I have no comrade,
    not even the lone man's friend –
Her who suffereth long and is kind;
    accepts what he is too weak to mend:
Down there they are dubious and askance;
    there nobody thinks as I,
But mind-chains do not clank
    where one's next neighbour is the sky.

In the towns I am tracked by phantoms
    having weird detective ways –
Shadows of beings who fellowed
    with myself of earlier days:

They hang about at places, and they say
    harsh heavy things –
Men with a wintry sneer, and women
    with tart disparagings.

Down there I seem to be false to myself,
    my simple self that was,
And is not now, and I see him watching,
    wondering what crass cause
Can have merged him into such a strange
    continuator as this,
Who yet has something in common with himself,
    my chrysalis.

I cannot go to the great gray Plain;
    there's a figure against the moon,
Nobody sees it but I, and it makes my breast
    beat out of tune;
I cannot go to the tall-spired town, being barred
    by the forms now passed
For everybody but me, in whose long vision
    they stand there fast.

There's a ghost at Yell'ham Bottom chiding loud
    at the fall of the night,
There's a ghost in Froom-side Vale,
    thin lipped and vague, in a shroud of white,

There is one in the railway-train
  whenever I do not want it near,
I see its profile against the pane,
  saying what I would not hear.

As for one rare fair woman, I am now
  but a thought of hers,
I enter her mind and another thought succeeds me
  that she prefers;
Yet my love for her in its fulness she herself
  even did not know;
Well, time cures hearts of tenderness,
  and now I can let her go.

So I am found on Ingpen Beacon,
  or on Wylls-Neck to the west,
Or else on homely Bulbarrow, or little Pilsdon Crest,
Where men have never cared to haunt,
  nor women have walked with me,
And ghosts then keep their distance;
  and I know some liberty.

OLD FURNITURE

I know not how it may be with others
    Who sit amid relics of householdry
That date from the days of their mothers' mothers,
    But well I know how it is with me
        Continually.

I see the hands of the generations
    That owned each shiny familiar thing
In play on its knobs and indentations,
    And with its ancient fashioning
        Still dallying:

Hands behind hands, growing paler and paler,
    As in a mirror a candle-flame
Shows images of itself, each frailer
    As it recedes, though the eye may frame
        Its shape the same.

On the clock's dull dial a foggy finger,
    Moving to set the minutes right
With tentative touches that lift and linger
    In the wont of a moth on a summer night,
        Creeps to my sight.

On this old viol, too, fingers are dancing –
    As whilom – just over the strings by the nut,
The tip of a bow receding, advancing
    In airy quivers, as if it would cut
        The plaintive gut.

And I see a face by that box for tinder,
    Glowing forth in fits from the dark,
And fading again, as the linten cinder
    Kindles to red at the flinty spark,
        Or goes out stark.

Well, well. It is best to be up and doing,
    The world has no use for one to-day
Who eyes things thus – no aim pursuing!
    He should not continue in this stay,
        But sink away.

THE PEDIGREE

I

I bent in the deep of night
Over a pedigree the chronicler gave
As mine; and as I bent there, half-unrobed,
The uncurtained panes of my window-square
   let in the watery light
      Of the moon in its old age:
And green-rheumed clouds were hurrying past
      where mute and cold it globed
   Like a drifting dolphin's eye seen through
      a lapping wave.

II

So, scanning my sire-sown tree,
   And the hieroglyphs of this spouse tied to that,
With offspring mapped below in lineage,
   Till the tangles troubled me,
The branches seemed to twist into a seared
      and cynic face
   Which winked and tokened towards the window
         like a Mage
      Enchanting me to gaze again thereat.

III

It was a mirror now,
And in it a long perspective I could trace
Of my begetters, dwindling backward each past each
All with the kindred look,
Whose names had since been inked down
in their place
On the recorder's book,
Generation and generation of my mien, and build,
and brow.

IV

And then did I divine
That every heave and coil and move I made
Within my brain, and in my mood and speech,
Was in the glass portrayed
As long forestalled by their so making it;
The first of them, the primest fuglemen
of my line,
Being fogged in far antiqueness past surmise
and reason's reach.

V

Said I then, sunk in tone,
'I am merest mimicker and counterfeit! –
Though thinking, *I am I,*
And what I do I do myself alone.'
 – The cynic twist of the page thereat unknit
Back to its normal figure,
having wrought its purport wry,
The Mage's mirror left the window-square,
And the stained moon and drift retook
their places there.

1916

DOMICILIUM

It faces west, and round the back and sides
High beeches, bending, hang a veil of boughs,
And sweep against the roof. Wild honeysucks
Climb on the walls, and seem to sprout a wish
(If we may fancy wish of trees and plants)
To overtop the apple-trees hard by.

Red roses, lilacs, variegated box
Are there in plenty, and such hardy flowers
As flourish best untrained. Adjoining these
Are herbs and esculents; and farther still
A field; then cottages with trees, and last
The distant hills and sky.

Behind, the scene is wilder. Heath and furze
Are everything that seems to grow and thrive
Upon the uneven ground. A stunted thorn
Stands here and there, indeed; and from a pit
An oak uprises, springing from a seed
Dropped by some bird a hundred years ago.

                              In days bygone –
Long gone – my father's mother, who is now
Blest with the blest, would take me out to walk.
At such a time I once inquired of her
How looked the spot when first she settled here.
The answer I remember. 'Fifty years
Have passed since then, my child,
          and change has marked
The face of all things. Yonder garden-plots
And orchards were uncultivated slopes
O'ergrown with bramble bushes, furze and thorn:
That road a narrow path shut in by ferns,
Which, almost trees, obscured the passer-by.

'Our house stood quite alone, and those tall firs
And beeches were not planted. Snakes and efts
Swarmed in the summer days, and nightly bats
Would fly about our bedrooms. Heathcroppers
Lived on the hills, and were our only friends;
So wild it was when first we settled here.'

ON THE DOORSTEP

The rain imprinted the step's wet shine
With target-circles that quivered and crossed
As I was leaving this porch of mine;
When from within there swelled and paused
            A song's sweet note;
        And back I turned, and thought,
            'Here I'll abide.'

The step shines wet beneath the rain,
Which prints its circles as heretofore;
I watch them from the porch again,
But no song-notes within the door
            Now call to me
        To shun the dripping lea;
            And forth I stride.

JANUARY 1914

MOMENTS OF VISION

MOMENTS OF VISION

That mirror
Which makes of men a transparency,
Who holds that mirror
And bids us such a breast-bare spectacle see
Of you and me?

That mirror
Whose magic penetrates like a dart,
Who lifts that mirror
And throws our mind back on us, and our heart,
Until we start?

That mirror
Works well in these night hours of ache;
Why in that mirror
Are tincts we never see ourselves once take
When the world is awake?

That mirror
Can test each mortal when unaware;
Yea, that strange mirror
May catch his last thoughts, whole life foul or fair
Glassing it – where?

THE SELF-UNSEEING

Here is the ancient floor,
Footworn and hollowed and thin,
Here was the former door
Where the dead feet walked in.

She sat here in her chair,
Smiling into the fire;
He who played stood there,
Bowing it higher and higher.

Childlike, I danced in a dream;
Blessings emblazoned that day;
Everything glowed with a gleam;
Yet we were looking away!

ON THE ESPLANADE
MIDSUMMER: 10 P.M.

The broad bald moon edged up
    where the sea was wide,
        Mild, mellow-faced;
Beneath, a tumbling twinkle of shines, like dyed,
        A trackway traced
To the shore, as of petals fallen from a rose to waste,
        In its overblow,
And fluttering afloat on inward heaves of the tide: –
All this, so plain; yet the rest I did not know.

The horizon gets lost in a mist new-wrought
    by the night:
        The lamps of the Bay
That reach from behind me round to the left and right
        On the sea-wall way
For a constant mile of curve, make a long display
        As a pearl-strung row,
Under which in the waves
    they bore their gimlets of light: –
All this was plain; but there was a thing not so.

Inside a window, open, with undrawn blind,
     There plays and sings
A lady unseen a melody undefined:
     And where the moon flings
Its shimmer a vessel crosses, whereon to the strings
     Plucked sweetly and low
Of a harp, they dance. Yea, such did I mark.
     That, behind,
My Fate's masked face crept near me I did not know!

THE SECOND VISIT

Clack, clack, clack, went the mill-wheel as I came,
And she was on the bridge with the thin hand-rail,
And the miller at the door, and the ducks at mill-tail;
I come again years after, and all there seems the same.

    And so indeed it is: the apple-tree'd old house,
And the deep mill-pond, and the wet wheel clacking,
And a woman on the bridge, and white ducks quacking,
And the miller at the door, powdered pale
        from boots to brows.

But it's not the same miller whom long ago I knew,
Nor are they the same apples, nor the same drops
        that dash
Over the wet wheel, nor the ducks below that splash,
Nor the woman who to fond plaints replied,
        'You know I do!'

BEREFT

In the black winter morning
No light will be struck near my eyes
While the clock in the stairway is warning
For five, when he used to rise.
   Leave the door unbarred,
   The clock unwound,
   Make my lone bed hard –
   Would 'twere underground!

When the summer dawns clearly,
And the appletree-tops seem alight,
Who will undraw the curtain and cheerly
Call out that the morning is bright?

When I tarry at market
No form will cross Durnover Lea
In the gathering darkness, to hark at
Grey's Bridge for the pit-pat o' me.

When the supper crock's steaming,
And the time is the time of his tread,
I shall sit by the fire and wait dreaming
In a silence as of the dead.
        Leave the door unbarred,
        The clock unwound,
        Make my lone bed hard –
        Would 'twere underground!

1901

NEUTRAL TONES

We stood by a pond that winter day,
And the sun was white, as though chidden of God,
And a few leaves lay on the starving sod;
  – They had fallen from an ash, and were gray.

Your eyes on me were as eyes that rove
Over tedious riddles of years ago;
And some words played between us to and fro
  On which lost the more by our love.

The smile on your mouth was the deadest thing
Alive enough to have strength to die;
And a grin of bitterness swept thereby
  Like an ominous bird a-wing . . .

Since then, keen lessons that love deceives,
And wrings with wrong, have shaped to me
Your face, and the God-curst sun, and a tree,
  And a pond edged with grayish leaves.

1867

TWO LIPS

I kissed them in fancy as I came
    Away in the morning glow;
I kissed them through the glass of her picture-frame:
    She did not know.

I kissed them in love, in troth, in laughter,
    When she knew all; long so!
That I should kiss them in a shroud thereafter
    She did not know.

AT MIDDLE-FIELD GATE IN FEBRUARY

The bars are thick with drops that show
    As they gather themselves from the fog
Like silver buttons ranged in a row,
And as evenly spaced as if measured, although
    They fall at the feeblest jog.

They load the leafless hedge hard by,
    And the blades of last year's grass,
While the fallow ploughland turned up nigh
In raw rolls, clammy and clogging lie –
    Too clogging for feet to pass.

How dry it was on a far-back day
    When straws hung the hedge and around,
When amid the sheaves in amorous play
In curtained bonnets and light array
    Bloomed a bevy now underground!

BOCKHAMPTON LANE

NIGHT-TIME IN MID-FALL

It is a storm-strid night, winds footing swift
    Through the blind profound;
  I know the happenings from their sound;
Leaves totter down still green, and spin and drift;
The tree-trunks rock to their roots,
    which wrench and lift
The loam where they run onward underground.

The streams are muddy and swollen; eels migrate
    To a new abode;
  Even cross, 'tis said, the turnpike-road;
(Men's feet have felt their crawl, home-coming late):
The westward fronts of towers are saturate,
Church-timbers crack, and witches ride abroad.

A LIGHT SNOW-FALL AFTER FROST

On the flat road a man at last appears:
      How much his whitening hairs
Owe to the settling snow's mute anchorage,
And how much to life's rough pilgrimage,
      One cannot certify.

      The frost is on the wane,
And cobwebs hanging close outside the pane
Pose as festoons of thick white worsted there,
Of their pale presence no eye being aware
      Till the rime made them plain.

      A second man comes by;
His ruddy beard brings fire to the pallid scene:
      His coat is faded green;
      Hence seems it that his mien
      Wears something of the dye
Of the berried holm-trees that he passes nigh.

The snow-feathers so gently sweep that though
      But half an hour ago
The road was brown, and now is starkly white,
A watcher would have failed defining quite
      When it transformed it so.

NEAR SURBITON

SNOW IN THE SUBURBS

Every branch big with it,
Bent every twig with it;
Every fork like a white web-foot;
Every street and pavement mute:
Some flakes have lost their way, and grope back
upward, when
Meeting those meandering down they turn and
descend again.
The palings are glued together like a wall,
And there is no waft of wind with the fleecy fall.

A sparrow enters the tree,
Whereon immediately
A snow-lump thrice his own slight size
Descends on him and
showers his head and eyes,
And overturns him,
And near inurns him,
And lights on a nether twig, when its brush
Starts off a volley of other lodging lumps with a rush.

The steps are a blanched slope,
Up which, with feeble hope,
A black cat comes, wide-eyed and thin;
And we take him in.

MUSIC IN A SNOWY STREET

The weather is sharp,
But the girls are unmoved:
One wakes from a harp,
The next from a viol,
A strain that I loved
When life was no trial.

The tripletime beat
Bounds forth on the snow,
But the spry springing feet
Of a century ago,
And the arms that enlaced
As the couples embraced,
Are silent old bones
Under graying gravestones.

The snow-feathers sail
Across the harp-strings,
Whose throbbing threads wail
Like love-satiate things.
Each lyre's grimy mien,
With its rout-raising tune,
Against the new white
Of the flake-laden noon,
Is incongruous to sight,

Hinting years they have seen
Of revel at night
Ere these damsels became
Possessed of their frame.

O bygone whirls, heys,
Crotchets, quavers, the same
That were danced in the days
Of grim Bonaparte's fame,
Or even by the toes
Of the fair Antoinette, –
Yea, old notes like those
Here are living on yet! –
But of their fame and fashion
How little these know
Who strum without passion
For pence, in the snow!

A MERRYMAKING IN QUESTION

'I will get a new string for my fiddle,
    And call to the neighbours to come,
And partners shall dance down the middle
    Until the old pewter-wares hum:
    And we'll sip the mead, cyder, and rum!'

From the night came the oddest of answers:
    A hollow wind, like a bassoon,
And headstones all ranged up as dancers,
    And cypresses droning a croon,
    And gurgoyles that mouthed to the tune.

MIDDLE-AGE ENTHUSIASMS

We passed where flag and flower
Signalled a jocund throng;
We said: 'Go to, the hour
Is apt!' – and joined the song;
And, kindling, laughed at life and care,
Although we knew no laugh lay there.

We walked where shy birds stood
Watching us, wonder-dumb;
Their friendship met our mood;
We cried: 'We'll often come:
We'll come morn, noon, eve, everywhen!'
– We doubted we should come again.

We joyed to see strange sheens
Leap from quaint leaves in shade;
A secret light of greens
They'd for their pleasure made.
We said: 'We'll set such sorts as these!'
– We knew with night the wish would cease.

'So sweet the place,' we said,
'Its tacit tales so dear,
Our thoughts, when breath has sped,
Will meet and mingle here!' ...
'Words!' mused we. 'Passed the mortal door,
Our thoughts will reach this nook no more.'

THE NIGHT OF THE DANCE

The cold moon hangs to the sky by its horn,
    And centres its gaze on me;
The stars, like eyes in reverie,
Their westering as for a while forborne,
    Quiz downward curiously.

Old Robert draws the backbrand in,
    The green logs steam and spit;
The half-awakened sparrows flit
From the riddled thatch; and owls begin
    To whoo from the gable-slit.

Yes; far and nigh things seem to know
    Sweet scenes are impending here;
That all is prepared; that the hour is near
For welcomes, fellowships, and flow
    Of sally, song, and cheer;

That spigots are pulled and viols strung;
    That soon will arise the sound
Of measures trod to tunes renowned;
That She will return in Love's low tongue
    My vows as we wheel around.

AT DAY-CLOSE IN NOVEMBER

The ten hours' light is abating,
      And a late bird wings across,
Where the pines, like waltzers waiting,
      Give their black heads a toss.

Beech leaves, that yellow the noon-time,
      Float past like specks in the eye;
I set every tree in my June time,
      And now they obscure the sky.

And the children who ramble through here
      Conceive that there never has been
A time when no tall trees grew here,
      That none will in time be seen.

MIDNIGHT ON THE GREAT WESTERN

In the third-class seat sat the journeying boy,
    And the roof-lamp's oily flame
Played down on his listless form and face,
Bewrapt past knowing to what he was going,
       Or whence he came.

In the band of his hat the journeying boy
    Had a ticket stuck; and a string
Around his neck bore the key of his box,
That twinkled gleams of the lamp's sad beams
      Like a living thing.

What past can be yours, O journeying boy
    Towards a world unknown,
Who calmly, as if uncurious quite
On all at stake, can undertake
      This plunge alone?

Knows your soul a sphere, O journeying boy,
    Our rude realms far above,
Whence with spacious vision you mark and mete
This region of sin that you find you in,
      But are not of?

AN AUGUST MIDNIGHT

I

A shaded lamp and a waving blind,
And the beat of a clock from a distant floor:
On this scene enter – winged, horned, and spined –
A longlegs, a moth, and a dumbledore;
While 'mid my page there idly stands
A sleepy fly, that rubs its hands ...

II

Thus meet we five, in this still place,
At this point of time, at this point in space.
– My guests besmear my new-penned line,
Or bang at the lamp and fall supine.
'God's humblest, they!' I muse. Yet why?
They know Earth-secrets that know not I.

MAX GATE, 1899

AT THE ROYAL ACADEMY

These summer landscapes – clump, and copse,
    and croft –
Woodland and meadowland – here hung aloft,
Gay with limp grass and leafery new and soft,

Seem caught from the immediate season's yield
I saw last noonday shining over the field,
By rapid snatch, while still are uncongealed

The saps that in their live originals climb;
Yester's quick greenage here set forth in mime
Just as it stands, now, at our breathing-time.

But these young foils so fresh upon each tree,
Soft verdures spread in sprouting novelty,
Are not this summer's though they feign to be.

Last year their May to Michaelmas term was run,
Last autumn browned and buried every one,
And no more know they sight of any sun.

A CATHEDRAL FAÇADE AT MIDNIGHT

Along the sculptures of the western wall
    I watched the moonlight creeping:
It moved as if it hardly moved at all,
    Inch by inch thinly peeping
Round on the pious figures of freestone, brought
And poised there when the Universe was wrought
To serve its centre, Earth, in mankind's thought.

The lunar look skimmed scantly toe, breast, arm,
    Then edged on slowly, slightly,
To shoulder, hand, face; till each austere form
    Was blanched its whole length brightly
Of prophet, king, queen, cardinal in state,
That dead men's tools had striven to simulate;
And the stiff images stood irradiate.

A frail moan from the martyred saints there set
    Mid others of the erection
Against the breeze, seemed sighings of regret
    At the ancient faith's rejection
Under the sure, unhasting, steady stress
Of Reason's movement, making meaningless
The coded creeds of old-time godliness.

IN A CATHEDRAL CITY

These people have not heard your name;
No loungers in this placid place
Have helped to bruit your beauty's fame.

The gray Cathedral, towards whose face
Bend eyes untold, has met not yours;
Your shade has never swept its base,

Your form has never darked its doors,
Nor have your faultless feet once thrown
A pensive pit-pat on its floors.

Along the street to maids well known
Blithe lovers hum their tender airs,
But in your praise voice not a tone . . .

– Since nought bespeaks you here, or bears,
As I, your imprint through and through,
Here might I rest, till my heart shares
The spot's unconsciousness of you.

SALISBURY

61

SHUT OUT THAT MOON

Close up the casement, draw the blind,
    Shut out that stealing moon,
She wears too much the guise she wore
    Before our lutes were strewn
With years-deep dust, and names we read
    On a white stone were hewn.

Step not forth on the dew-dashed lawn
    To view the Lady's Chair,
Immense Orion's glittering form,
    The Less and Greater Bear:
Stay in; to such sights we were drawn
    When faded ones were fair.

Brush not the bough for midnight scents
   That come forth lingeringly,
And wake the same sweet sentiments
    They breathed to you and me.
When living seemed a laugh, and love
    All it was said to be.

Within the common lamp-lit room
    Prison my eyes and thought;
Let dingy details crudely loom,
    Mechanic speech be wrought:
Too fragrant was Life's early bloom,
    Too tart the fruit it brought!

1904

A SPELLBOUND PALACE
(HAMPTON COURT)

On this kindly yellow day
    of mild low-travelling winter sun
        The stirless depths of the yews
        Are vague with misty blues:
Across the spacious pathways
    stretching spires of shadow run,
And the wind-gnawed walls of ancient brick are fired
    vermilion.

        Two or three early sanguine finches tune
    Some tentative strains,
        to be enlarged by May or June:
           From a thrush or blackbird
           Comes now and then a word,
While an enfeebled fountain
    somewhere within is heard.

Our footsteps wait awhile,
Then draw beneath the pile,
When an inner court outspreads
As 'twere History's own asile,
Where the now-visioned fountain
    its attenuate crystal sheds
In passive lapse that seems to ignore
    the yon world's clamorous clutch,
And lays an insistent numbness on the place,
    like a cold hand's touch.

And there swaggers the Shade of a straddling King,
    plumed, sworded, with sensual face,
And lo, too, that of his Minister,
    at a bold self-centred pace:
Sheer in the sun they pass; and thereupon all is still,
Save the mindless fountain tinkling on
    with thin enfeebled will.

THE DARKLING THRUSH

I leant upon a coppice gate
    When Frost was spectre-gray,
And Winter's dregs made desolate
    The weakening eye of day.
The tangled bine-stems scored the sky
    Like strings of broken lyres,
And all mankind that haunted nigh
    Had sought their household fires.

The land's sharp features seemed to be
    The Century's corpse outleant,
His crypt the cloudy canopy,
    The wind his death-lament.
The ancient pulse of germ and birth
    Was shrunken hard and dry,
And every spirit upon earth
    Seemed fervourless as I.

At once a voice arose among
　　The bleak twigs overhead
In a full-hearted evensong
　　Of joy illimited;
An aged thrush, frail, gaunt, and small,
　　In blast-beruffled plume,
Had chosen thus to fling his soul
　　Upon the growing gloom.

So little cause for carolings
　　Of such ecstatic sound
Was written on terrestrial things
　　Afar or nigh around,
That I could think there trembled through
　　His happy good-night air
Some blessed Hope, whereof he knew
　　And I was unaware.

31 DECEMBER 1900

THE CAGED GOLDFINCH

Within a churchyard, on a recent grave,
     I saw a little cage
That jailed a goldfinch. All was silence save
     Its hops from stage to stage.

There was inquiry in its wistful eye,
     And once it tried to sing;
Of him or her who placed it there, and why,
     No one knew anything.

'I WATCHED A BLACKBIRD'

I watched a blackbird on a budding sycamore
One Easter Day, when sap was stirring twigs
    to the core;
  I saw his tongue, and crocus-coloured bill
  Parting and closing as he turned his trill;
  Then he flew down, seized on a stem of hay,
And upped to where his building scheme was
    under way,
As if so sure a nest were never shaped on spray.

PROUD SONGSTERS

The thrushes sing as the sun is going,
And the finches whistle in ones and pairs,
And as it gets dark loud nightingales
      In bushes
Pipe, as they can when April wears,
    As if all Time were theirs.

These are brand-new birds
    of twelve-months' growing,
Which a year ago, or less than twain,
No finches were, nor nightingales,
      Nor thrushes,
But only particles of grain,
    And earth, and air, and rain.

WEATHERS

I

This is the weather the cuckoo likes,
  And so do I;
When showers betumble the chestnut spikes,
  And nestlings fly:
And the little brown nightingale bills his best,
And they sit outside at 'The Travellers' Rest',
And maids come forth sprig-muslin drest,
And citizens dream of the south and west,
  And so do I.

II

This is the weather the shepherd shuns,
  And so do I;
When beeches drip in browns and duns,
  And thresh, and ply;
And hill-hid tides throb, throe on throe,
And meadow rivulets overflow,
And drops on gate-bars hang in a row,
And rooks in families homeward go,
  And so do I.

A BIRD-SCENE AT A RURAL DWELLING

When the inmate stirs, the birds retire discreetly
From the window-ledge,
    whereon they whistled sweetly
    And on the step of the door,
    In the misty morning hoar;
  But now the dweller is up they flee
  To the crooked neighbouring codlin-tree;
And when he comes fully forth they seek the garden,
And call from the lofty costard, as pleading pardon
    For shouting so near before
    In their joy at being alive: –
Meanwhile the hammering clock within goes five.

I know a domicile of brown and green,
Where for a hundred summers there have been
Just such enactments, just such daybreaks seen.

AUTUMN IN KING'S HINTOCK PARK

Here by the baring bough
   Raking up leaves,
Often I ponder how
   Springtime deceives, –
I, an old woman now,
   Raking up leaves.

Here in the avenue
   Raking up leaves,
Lords' ladies pass in view,
   Until one heaves
Sighs at life's russet hue,
   Raking up leaves!

Just as my shape you see
   Raking up leaves,
I saw, when fresh and free,
   Those memory weaves
Into gray ghosts by me,
   Raking up leaves.

Yet, Dear, though one may sigh,
    Raking up leaves,
New leaves will dance on high –
    Earth never grieves! –
Will not, when missed am I
    Raking up leaves.

1901

FRIENDS BEYOND

William Dewy, Tranter Reuben, Farmer Ledlow
    late at plough,
        Robert's kin, and John's, and Ned's,
And the Squire, and Lady Susan,
    lie in Mellstock churchyard now!

'Gone,' I call them, gone for good, that group
    of local hearts and heads;
        Yet at mothy curfew-tide,
And at midnight when the noon-heat breathes
    it back from walls and leads,

They've a way of whispering to me – fellow-wight who
    yet abide –
        In the muted, measured note
Of a ripple under archways, or a lone cave's stillicide:

'We have triumphed: this achievement turns
    the bane to antidote,
        Unsuccesses to success,
Many thought-worn eves and morrows
    to a morrow free of thought.

'No more need we corn and clothing,
　　feel of old terrestrial stress;
　　　　Chill detraction stirs no sigh;
Fear of death has even bygone us: death gave
　　all that we possess.'

W. D. – 'Ye mid burn the old bass-viol
　　that I set such value by.'
Squire. – 'You may hold the manse in fee,
　　You may wed my spouse, may let
　　　　my children's memory of me die.'

Lady S. – 'You may have my rich brocades, my laces;
　　take each household key;
　　　　Ransack coffer, desk, bureau;
　　Quiz the few poor treasures hid there,
　　　　con the letters kept by me.'

Far. – 'Ye mid zell my favourite heifer,
　　ye mid let the charlock grow,
　　　　Foul the grinterns, give up thrift.'
Far. Wife. – 'If ye break my best blue china, children,
　　I shan't care or ho.'

All. – 'We've no wish to hear the tidings,
      how the people's fortunes shift;
         What your daily doings are;
      Who are wedded, born, divided;
            if your lives beat slow or swift.

'Curious not the least are we if our intents
      you make or mar,
         If you quire to our old tune,
If the City stage still passes, if the weirs still roar afar.'

– Thus, with very gods' composure, freed those crosses
      late and soon
         Which, in life, the Trine allow
(Why, none witteth), and ignoring all that haps
      beneath the moon,

William Dewy, Tranter Reuben, Farmer Ledlow
      late at plough,
         Robert's kin, and John's, and Ned's,
And the Squire, and Lady Susan, murmur mildly
      to me now.

A BACKWARD SPRING

The trees are afraid to put forth buds,
And there is timidity in the grass;
The plots lie gray where gouged by spuds,
    And whether next week will pass
Free of sly sour winds is the fret of each bush
    Of barberry waiting to bloom.

Yet the snowdrop's face betrays no gloom,
And the primrose pants in its heedless push,
Though the myrtle asks if it's worth the fight
    This year with frost and rime
    To venture one more time

On delicate leaves and buttons of white
From the selfsame bough as at last year's prime,
And never to ruminate on or remember
What happened to it in mid-December.

APRIL 1917

SEVENTY-FOUR AND TWENTY

Here goes a man of seventy-four,
Who sees not what life means for him,
And here another in years a score
Who reads its very figure and trim.

The one who shall walk to-day with me
Is not the youth who gazes far,
But the breezy sire who cannot see
What Earth's ingrained conditions are.

GEORGE MEREDITH
(1828–1909)

Forty years aback, when much had place
That since has perished out of mind,
I heard that voice and saw that face.

He spoke as one afoot will wind
A morning horn ere men awake;
His note was trenchant, turning kind.

He was one of those whose wit can shake
And riddle to the very core
The counterfeits that Time will break . . .

Of late, when we two met once more,
The luminous countenance and rare
Shone just as forty years before.

So that, when now all tongues declare
His shape unseen by his green hill,
I scarce believe he sits not there.

No matter. Further and further still
Through the world's vaporous vitiate air
His words wing on – as live words will.

MAY 1909

ON THE PORTRAIT OF A WOMAN
ABOUT TO BE HANGED

Comely and capable one of our race,
Posing there in your gown of grace,
    Plain, yet becoming;
        Could subtlest breast
        Ever have guessed
What was behind that innocent face,
    Drumming, drumming!

Would that your Causer, ere knoll your knell
For this riot of passion, might deign to tell
    Why, since It made you
        Sound in the germ,
        It sent a worm
To madden Its handiwork, when It might well
    Not have assayed you,

Not have implanted, to your deep rue,
The Clytaemnestra spirit in you,
    And with purblind vision
        Sowed a tare
        In a field so fair,
And a thing of symmetry, seemly to view,
    Brought to derision!

6 JANUARY 1923

WIVES IN THE SERE

I

Never a careworn wife but shows,
    If a joy suffuse her,
Something beautiful to those
    Patient to peruse her,
Some one charm the world unknows
    Precious to a muser,
Haply what, ere years were foes,
    Moved her mate to choose her.

II

But, be it a hint of rose
    That an instant hues her,
Or some early light or pose
    Wherewith thought renews her –
Seen by him at full, ere woes
    Practised to abuse her –
Sparely comes it, swiftly goes,
    Time again subdues her.

NEAR LANIVET, 1872

There was a stunted handpost just on the crest,
    Only a few feet high:
She was tired, and we stopped in the twilight-time
    for her rest,
      At the crossways close thereby.

She leant back, being so weary, against its stem,
    And laid her arms on its own,
Each open palm stretched out to each end of them,
    Her sad face sideways thrown.

Her white-clothed form at this dim-lit cease of day
    Made her look as one crucified
In my gaze at her from the midst of the dusty way,
    And hurriedly 'Don't,' I cried.

I do not think she heard. Loosing thence she said,
    As she stepped forth ready to go,
'I am rested now. – Something strange
    came into my head;
      I wish I had not leant so!'

And wordless we moved onward down from the hill
    In the west cloud's murked obscure,
And looking back we could see the handpost still
    In the solitude of the moor.

'It struck her too,' I thought, for as if afraid
    She heavily breathed as we trailed;
Till she said, 'I did not think how 'twould look
    in the shade,
      When I leant there like one nailed.'

I, lightly: 'There's nothing in it. For *you* anyhow!'
    – 'O I know there is not,' said she . . .
  'Yet I wonder . . . If no one is bodily crucified now,
    In spirit one may be!'

And we dragged on and on, while we seemed to see
    In the running of Time's far glass
Her crucified, as she had wondered if she might be
    Some day. – Alas, alas!

IMAGININGS

She saw herself a lady
        With fifty frocks in wear,
And rolling wheels, and rooms the best,
        And faithful maidens' care,
    And open lawns and shady
        For weathers warm or drear.

She found herself a striver,
        All liberal gifts debarred,
With days of gloom, and movements stressed,
        And early visions marred,
    And got no man to wive her
        But one whose lot was hard.

Yet in the moony night-time
        She steals to stile and lea
During his heavy slumberous rest
        When homecome wearily,
    And dreams of some blest bright-time
        She knows can never be.

I LOOK INTO MY GLASS

I look into my glass,
And view my wasting skin,
And say, 'Would God it came to pass
My heart had shrunk as thin!'

For then, I, undistrest
By hearts grown cold to me,
Could lonely wait my endless rest
With equanimity.

But Time, to make me grieve,
Part steals, lets part abide;
And shakes this fragile frame at eve
With throbbings of noontide.

SATIRES OF
CIRCUMSTANCE

AT TEA

The kettle descants in a cosy drone,
And the young wife looks in her husband's face,
And then at her guest's, and shows in her own
Her sense that she fills an envied place;
And the visiting lady is all abloom,
And says there was never so sweet a room.

And the happy young housewife does not know
That the woman beside her was first his choice,
Till the fates ordained it could not be so . . .
Betraying nothing in look or voice
The guest sits smiling and sips her tea,
And he throws her a stray glance yearningly.

IN CHURCH

'And now to God the Father,' he ends,
And his voice thrills up to the topmost tiles:
Each listener chokes as he bows and bends,
And emotion pervades the crowded aisles.
Then the preacher glides to the vestry-door,
And shuts it, and thinks he is seen no more.

The door swings softly ajar meanwhile,
And a pupil of his in the Bible class,
Who adores him as one without gloss or guile,
Sees her idol stand with a satisfied smile
And re-enact at the vestry-glass
Each pulpit gesture in deft dumb-show
That had moved the congregation so.

BY HER AUNT'S GRAVE

'Sixpence a week', says the girl to her lover,
'Aunt used to bring me, for she could confide
In me alone, she vowed. 'Twas to cover
The cost of her headstone when she died.
And that was a year ago last June;
I've not yet fixed it. But I must soon.'

'And where is the money now, my dear?'
'O, snug in my purse ... Aunt was *so* slow
In saving it – eighty weeks, or near.' ...
'Let's spend it,' he hints. 'For she won't know.
There's a dance to-night at the Load of Hay.'
She passively nods. And they go that way.

IN THE ROOM OF THE BRIDE-ELECT

'Would it had been the man of our wish!'
Sighs her mother. To whom with vehemence she
In the wedding-dress – the wife to be –
'Then why were you so mollyish
As not to insist on him for me!'
The mother, amazed: 'Why, dearest one,
Because you pleaded for this or none!'

'But Father and you should have stood out strong!
Since then, to my cost, I have lived to find
That you were right and I was wrong;
This man is a dolt to the one declined. . . .
Ah! – here he comes with his button-hole rose.
Good God – I must marry him I suppose!'

AT A WATERING-PLACE

They sit and smoke on the esplanade,
The man and his friend, and regard the bay
Where the far chalk cliffs, to the left displayed,
Smile sallowly in the decline of day.
And saunterers pass with laugh and jest –
A handsome couple among the rest.

'That smart proud pair', says the man to his friend,
'Are to marry next week. . . . How little he thinks
That dozens of days and nights on end
I have stroked her neck, unhooked the links
Of her sleeve to get at her upper arm. . . .
Well, bliss is in ignorance: what's the harm!'

IN THE CEMETERY

'You see those mothers squabbling there?'
Remarks the man of the cemetery.
'One says in tears, " 'Tis mine lies here!"
Another, "Nay, mine, you Pharisee!"
Another, "How dare you move my flowers
And put your own on this grave of ours!"
But all the children were laid therein
At different times, like sprats in a tin.

'And then the main drain had to cross,
And we moved the lot some nights ago,
And packed them away in the general foss
With hundreds more. But their folks don't know,
And as well cry over a new-laid drain
As anything else, to ease your pain!'

OUTSIDE THE WINDOW

'My stick!' he says, and turns in the lane
To the house just left, whence a vixen voice
Comes out with the firelight through the pane,
And he sees within that the girl of his choice
Stands rating her mother with eyes aglare
For something said while he was there.

'At last I behold her soul undraped!'
Thinks the man who had loved her more than himself;
'My God! – 'tis but narrowly I have escaped. –
My precious porcelain proves it delf.'
His face has reddened like one ashamed,
And he steals off, leaving his stick unclaimed.

IN THE STUDY

He enters, and mute on the edge of a chair
Sits a thin-faced lady, a stranger there,
A type of decayed gentility;
And by some small signs he well can guess
That she comes to him almost breakfastless.

'I have called – I hope I do not err –
I am looking for a purchaser
Of some score volumes of the works
Of eminent divines I own, –
Left by my father – though it irks
My patience to offer them.' And she smiles
As if necessity were unknown;
'But the truth of it is that oftenwhiles
I have wished, as I am fond of art,
To make my rooms a little smart,
And these old books are so in the way.'
And lightly still she laughs to him,
As if to sell were a mere gay whim,
And that, to be frank, Life were indeed
To her not vinegar and gall,
But fresh and honey-like; and Need
No household skeleton at all.

AT THE ALTAR-RAIL

'My bride is not coming, alas!' says the groom,
And the telegram shakes in his hand. 'I own
It was hurried! We met at a dancing-room
When I went to the Cattle-Show alone,
And then, next night, where the Fountain leaps,
And the Street of the Quarter-Circle sweeps.

'Ay, she won me to ask her to be my wife –
'Twas foolish perhaps! – to forsake the ways
Of the flaring town for a farmer's life.
She agreed. And we fixed it. Now she says:
"It's sweet of you, dear, to prepare me a nest,
But a swift, short gay life suits me best.
What I really am you have never gleaned;
I had eaten the apple ere you were weaned." '

IN THE NUPTIAL CHAMBER

'O that mastering tune!' And up in the bed
Like a lace-robed phantom springs the bride;
'And why?' asks the man she had that day wed,
With a start, as the band plays on outside.
'It's the townsfolks' cheery compliment
Because of our marriage, my Innocent.'

'O but you don't know! 'Tis the passionate air
To which my old Love waltzed with me,
And I swore as we spun that none should share
My home, my kisses, till death, save he!
And he dominates me and thrills me through,
And it's he I embrace while embracing you!'

IN THE RESTAURANT

'But hear. If you stay, and the child be born,
It will pass as your husband's with the rest,
While, if we fly, the teeth of scorn
Will be gleaming at us from east to west;
And the child will come as a life despised;
I feel an elopement is ill-advised!'

'O you realize not what it is, my dear,
To a woman! Daily and hourly alarms
Lest the truth should out. How can I stay here,
And nightly take him into my arms!
Come to the child no name or fame,
Let's go, and face it, and bear the shame.'

AT THE DRAPER'S

'I stood at the back of the shop, my dear,
	But you did not perceive me.
Well, when they deliver what you were shown
	I shall know nothing of it, believe me!'

And he coughed and coughed as she paled and said,
	'O, I didn't see you come in there –
Why couldn't you speak?' – 'Well, I didn't. I left
	That you should not notice I'd been there.

'You were viewing some lovely things. *"Soon required*
	For a widow, of latest fashion";
And I knew 'twould upset you to meet the man
	Who had to be cold and ashen

'And screwed in a box before they could dress you
	"In the last new note in mourning",
As they defined it. So, not to distress you,
	I left you to your adorning.'

ON THE DEATH-BED

'I'll tell – being past all praying for –
Then promptly die. . . . He was out at the war,
And got some scent of the intimacy
That was under way between her and me;

'And he stole back home, and appeared like a ghost
One night, at the very time almost
That I reached her house. Well, I shot him dead,
And secretly buried him. Nothing was said.

'The news of the battle came next day;
He was scheduled missing. I hurried away,
Got out there, visited the field,
And sent home word that a search revealed
He was one of the slain; though, lying alone
And stript, his body had not been known.

'But she suspected. I lost her love,
Yea, my hope of earth, and of Heaven above;
And my time's now come, and I'll pay the score.
Though it be burning for evermore.'

OVER THE COFFIN

They stand confronting, the coffin between,
His wife of old, and his wife of late,
And the dead man whose they both had been
Seems listening aloof, as to things past date.
– 'I have called,' says the first. 'Do you marvel or not?'
'In truth,' says the second, 'I do – somewhat.'

'Well, there was a word to be said by me! . . .
I divorced that man because of you –
It seemed I must do it, boundenly;
But now I am older, and tell you true,
For life is little, and dead lies he;
I would I had let alone you two!
And both of us, scorning parochial ways,
Had lived like the wives in the patriarchs' days.'

IN THE MOONLIGHT

'O lonely workman, standing there
In a dream, why do you stare and stare
At her grave, as no other grave there were?

'If your great gaunt eyes so importune
Her soul by the shine of this corpse-cold moon,
Maybe you'll raise her phantom soon!'

'Why, fool, it is what I would rather see
Than all the living folk there be;
But alas, there is no such joy for me!'

'Ah – she was one you loved, no doubt,
Through good and evil, through rain and drought,
And when she passed, all your sun went out?'

'Nay: she was the woman I did not love,
Whom all the others were ranked above,
Whom during her life I thought nothing of.'

SHORT STORIES

THE PHOTOGRAPH

The flame crept up the portrait line by line
As it lay on the coals in the silence of night's profound,
    And over the arm's incline,
And along the marge of the silkwork superfine,
And gnawed at the delicate bosom's defenceless round.

Then I vented a cry of hurt, and averted my eyes;
The spectacle was one that I could not bear,
    To my deep and sad surprise;
But, compelled to heed, I again looked furtivewise
Till the flame had eaten her breasts, and mouth,
    and hair.

'Thank God, she is out of it now!' I said at last,
In a great relief of heart when the thing was done
    That had set my soul aghast,
And nothing was left of the picture
    unsheathed from the past
But the ashen ghost of the card it had figured on.

She was a woman long hid amid packs of years,
She might have been living or dead; she was lost
    to my sight,
        And the deed that had nigh drawn tears
Was done in a casual clearance of life's arrears;
But I felt as if I had put her to death that night!...

                *   *   *

– Well; she knew nothing thereof did she survive,
And suffered nothing if numbered among the dead;
        Yet – yet – if on earth alive
Did she feel a smart, and with vague strange
    anguish strive?
If in heaven, did she smile at me sadly
    and shake her head?

THE MOUND

     For a moment pause:-
     Just here it was;
And through the thin thorn hedge,
     by the rays of the moon,
I can see the tree in the field, and beside it the mound –
Now sheeted with snow – whereon we sat that June
     When it was green and round,
And she crazed my mind by what she coolly told –
     The history of her undoing,
(As I saw it), but she called 'comradeship',
     That bred in her no rueing:
     And saying she'd not be bound

For life to one man, young, ripe-yeared, or old,
Left me – an innocent simpleton to her viewing;
For, though my accompt of years outscored her own,
     Hers had more hotly flown . . .
We never met again by this green mound,
To press as once so often lip on lip,
       And palter, and pause:-
       Yes; here it was!

THE CHOIRMASTER'S BURIAL

He often would ask us
That, when he died,
After playing so many
To their last rest,
If out of us any
Should here abide,
And it would not task us,
We would with our lutes
Play over him
By his grave-brim
The psalm he liked best –
The one whose sense suits
'Mount Ephraim' –
And perhaps we should seem
To him, in Death's dream,
Like the seraphim.

As soon as I knew
That his spirit was gone
I thought this his due,
And spoke thereupon.
'I think,' said the vicar,
'A read service quicker
Than viols out-of-doors
In these frosts and hoars.

That old-fashioned way
Requires a fine day,
And it seems to me
It had better not be.'

Hence, that afternoon,
Though never knew he
That his wish could not be,
To get through it faster
They buried the master
Without any tune.

But 'twas said that, when
At the dead of next night
The vicar looked out,
There struck on his ken
Thronged roundabout,
Where the frost was graying
The headstoned grass,
A band all in white
Like the saints in church-glass,
Singing and playing
The ancient stave
By the choirmaster's grave.

Such the tenor man told
When he had grown old.

SEEN BY THE WAITS

Through snowy woods and shady
   We went to play a tune
To the lonely manor-lady
   By the light of the Christmas moon.

We violed till, upward glancing
   To where a mirror leaned,
It showed her airily dancing,
   Deeming her movements screened;

Dancing alone in the room there,
   Thin-draped in her robe of night;
Her postures, glassed in the gloom there,
   Were a strange phantasmal sight.

She had learnt (we heard when homing)
   That her roving spouse was dead:
Why she had danced in the gloaming
   We thought, but never said.

THE ENEMY'S PORTRAIT

He saw the portrait of his enemy, offered
At auction in a street he journeyed nigh,
That enemy, now late dead, who in his lifetime
Had injured deeply him the passer-by.
'To get that picture, pleased be God, I'll try,
And utterly destroy it; and no more
Shall be inflicted on man's mortal eye
A countenance so sinister and sore!'

And so he bought the painting. Driving homeward,
'The frame will come in useful,' he declared,
'The rest is fuel.' On his arrival, weary,
Asked what he bore with him, and how he fared,
He said he had bid for a picture, though he cared
For the frame only: on the morrow he
Would burn the canvas, which could well be spared,
Seeing that it portrayed his enemy.

Next day some other duty found him busy:
The foe was laid his face against the wall;
But on the next he set himself to loosen
The straining-strips. And then a casual call
Prevented his proceeding therewithal;
And thus the picture waited, day by day,
Its owner's pleasure, like a wretched thrall,
Until a month and more had slipped away.

And then upon a morn he found it shifted,
Hung in a corner by a servitor.
'Why did you take on you to hang that picture?
You know it was the frame I bought it for.'
'It stood in the way of every visitor,
And I just hitched it there.' – 'Well, it must go:
I don't commemorate men whom I abhor.
Remind me 'tis to do. The frame I'll stow.'

But things become forgotten. In the shadow
Of the dark corner hung it by its string,
And there it stayed – once noticed by its owner,
Who said, 'Ah me – I must destroy that thing!'
But when he died, there, none remembering,
It hung, till moved to prominence, as one sees;
And comers pause and say, examining,
'I thought they were the bitterest enemies?'

THE RIVAL

I determined to find out whose it was –
    The portrait he looked at so, and sighed;
Bitterly have I rued my meanness
        And wept for it since he died!

I searched his desk when he was away,
    And there was the likeness – yes, my own!
Taken when I was the season's fairest,
        And time-lines all unknown.

I smiled at my image, and put it back,
    And he went on cherishing it, until
I was chafed that he loved not the me then living,
        But that past woman still.

Well, such was my jealousy at last,
    I destroyed that face of the former me;
Could you ever have dreamed the heart of woman
        Would work so foolishly!

'A GENTLEMAN'S SECOND-HAND SUIT'

Here it is hanging in the sun
      By the pawn-shop door,
A dress-suit – all its revels done
      Of heretofore.
Long drilled to the waltzer's swing and sway,
      As its tokens show:
What it has seen, what it could say
      If it did but know!

The sleeve bears still a print of powder
      Rubbed from her arms
When she warmed up as the notes swelled louder
      And livened her charms –
Or rather theirs, for beauties many
      Leant there, no doubt,
Leaving these tell-tale traces when he
      Spun them about.

Its cut seems rather in bygone style
      On looking close,
So it mayn't have bent it for some while
      To the dancing pose:
Anyhow, often within its clasp
      Fair partners hung,
Assenting to the wearer's grasp
      With soft sweet tongue.

Where is, alas, the gentleman
      Who wore this suit?
And where are his ladies? Tell none can:
      Gossip is mute.
Some of them may forget him quite
      Who smudged his sleeve,
Some think of a wild and whirling night
      With him, and grieve.

DRUMMER HODGE

I

They throw in Drummer Hodge, to rest
    Uncoffined – just as found:
His landmark is a kopje-crest
    That breaks the veldt around;
And foreign constellations west
    Each night above his mound.

II

Young Hodge the Drummer never knew –
    Fresh from his Wessex home –
The meaning of the broad Karoo,
    The Bush, the dusty loam,
And why uprose to nightly view
    Strange stars amid the gloam.

III

Yet portion of that unknown plain
    Will Hodge for ever be;
His homely Northern breast and brain
    Grow to some Southern tree,
And strange-eyed constellations reign
    His stars eternally.

THE WORKBOX

'See, here's the workbox, little wife,
   That I made of polished oak.'
He was a joiner, of village life;
   She came of borough folk.

He holds the present up to her
   As with a smile she nears
And answers to the profferer,
   "Twill last all my sewing years!'

'I warrant it will. And longer too.
   'Tis a scantling that I got
Off poor John Wayward's coffin, who
   Died of they knew not what.

'The shingled pattern that seems to cease
   Against your box's rim
Continues right on in the piece
   That's underground with him.

'And while I worked it made me think
   Of timber's varied doom;
One inch where people eat and drink,
   The next inch in a tomb.

'But why do you look so white, my dear,
    And turn aside your face?
You knew not that good lad, I fear,
    Though he came from your native place?'

'How could I know that good young man,
    Though he came from my native town,
When he must have left far earlier than
    I was a woman grown?'

'Ah, no. I should have understood!
    It shocked you that I gave
To you one end of a piece of wood
    Whose other is in a grave?'

'Don't, dear, despise my intellect,
    Mere accidental things
Of that sort never have effect
    On my imaginings.'

Yet still her lips were limp and wan,
    Her face still held aside,
As if she had known not only John,
    But known of what he died.

HER SECOND HUSBAND HEARS
HER STORY

'Still, Dear, it is incredible to me
      That here, alone,
You should have sewed him up until he died,
And in this very bed. I do not see
How you could do it, seeing what might betide.'

'Well, he came home one midnight, liquored deep –
      Worse than I'd known –
And lay down heavily, and soundly slept:
Then, desperate driven, I thought of it, to keep
Him from me when he woke. Being an adept

'With needle and thimble, as he snored, click-click
      An hour I'd sewn,
Till, had he roused, he couldn't have moved from bed,
So tightly laced in sheet and quilt and tick
He lay. And in the morning he was dead.

'Ere people came I drew the stitches out,
      And thus 'twas shown
To be a stroke.' – 'It's a strange tale!' said he.
'And this same bed?' – 'Yes, here it came about.'
'Well, it sounds strange – told here and now to me.

'Did you intend his death by your tight lacing?'
      'O, that I cannot own.
I could not think of else that would avail
When he should wake up, and attempt embracing.' –
      'Well, it's a cool queer tale!'

SHE HEARS THE STORM

There was a time in former years –
    While my roof-tree was his –
When I should have been distressed by fears
    At such a night as this!

I should have murmured anxiously,
    'The pricking rain strikes cold;
His road is bare of hedge or tree,
    And he is getting old.'

But now the fitful chimney-roar,
    The drone of Thorncombe trees,
The Froom in flood upon the moor,
    The mud of Mellstock Leaze,

The candle slanting sooty-wick'd,
    The thuds upon the thatch,
The eaves-drops on the window flicked,
    The clacking garden-hatch,

And what they mean to wayfarers,
    I scarcely heed or mind;
He has won that storm-tight roof of hers
    Which Earth grants all her kind.

JUBILATE

'The very last time I ever was here,' he said,
'I saw much less of the quick than I saw of the dead.'
– He was a man I had met with somewhere before,
But how or when I now could recall no more.

'The hazy mazy moonlight at one in the morning
Spread out as a sea across the frozen snow,
Glazed to live sparkles
        like the great breastplate adorning
The priest of the Temple,
        with Urim and Thummim aglow.

'The yew-tree arms, glued hard to the stiff stark air,
Hung still in the village sky as theatre-scenes
When I came by the churchyard wall, and halted there
At a shut-in sound of fiddles and tambourines.

'And as I stood hearkening, dulcimers, hautboys,
        and shawms,
And violoncellos, and a three-stringed double-bass,
Joined in, and were intermixed
        with a singing of psalms;
And I looked over at the dead men's dwelling-place.

'Through the shine of the slippery snow
    I now could see,
As it were through a crystal roof, a great company
Of the dead minueting in stately step underground
To the tune of the instruments
    I had before heard sound.

'It was "Eden New", and dancing they sang in a chore,
"We are out of it all! – yea, in Little-Ease
    cramped no more!"
And their shrouded figures pacing with joy I could see
As you see the stage from the gallery.
    And they had no heed of me.

'And I lifted my head quite dazed
    from the churchyard wall
And I doubted not that it warned
    I should soon have my call.
But –' . . . Then in the ashes he emptied
    the dregs of his cup,
And onward he went, and the darkness
    swallowed him up.

A SHEEP FAIR

The day arrives of the autumn fair,
        And torrents fall,
Though sheep in throngs are gathered there,
        Ten thousand all,
Sodden, with hurdles round them reared:
And, lot by lot, the pens are cleared,
And the auctioneer wrings out his beard,
And wipes his book, bedrenched and smeared,
And rakes the rain from his face with the edge of his hand,
        As torrents fall.

The wool of the ewes is like a sponge
        With the daylong rain:
Jammed tight, to turn, or lie, or lunge,
        They strive in vain.
Their horns are soft as finger-nails,
Their shepherds reek against the rails,
The tied dogs soak with tucked-in tails,
The buyers' hat-brims fill like pails,
Which spill small cascades when they shift their stand
        In the daylong rain.

Time has trailed lengthily since met
    At Pummery Fair
Those panting thousands in their wet
    And woolly wear:
And every flock long since has bled,
And all the dripping buyers have sped,
And the hoarse auctioneer is dead,
Who 'Going – going!' so often said,
As he consigned to doom each meek, mewed band
    At Pummery Fair.

AN UNKINDLY MAY

A shepherd stands by a gate in a white smock-frock:
He holds the gate ajar, intently counting his flock.

The sour spring wind is blurting boisterous-wise,
And bears on it dirty clouds across the skies;
Plantation timbers creak like rusty cranes,
And pigeons and rooks, dishevelled by late rains,
Are like gaunt vultures, sodden and unkempt,
And song-birds do not end what they attempt:
The buds have tried to open, but quite failing
Have pinched themselves together in their quailing.
The sun frowns whitely in eye-trying flaps
Through passing cloud-holes, mimicking audible taps.
'Nature, you're not commendable to-day!'
I think. 'Better to-morrow!' she seems to say.

That shepherd still stands in that white smock-frock,
Unnoting all things save the counting his flock.

APOSTROPHE TO AN OLD PSALM TUNE

I met you first – ah, when did I first meet you?
When I was full of wonder, and innocent,
Standing meek-eyed with those of choric bent,
    While dimming day grew dimmer
        In the pulpit-glimmer.

Much riper in years I met you – in a temple
Where summer sunset streamed upon our shapes,
And you spread over me like a gauze that drapes,
    And flapped from floor to rafters,
        Sweet as angels' laughters.

But you had been stripped of some of your old vesture
By Monk, or another. Now you wore no frill,
And at first you startled me. But I knew you still,
    Though I missed the minim's waver,
        And the dotted quaver.

I grew accustomed to you thus. And you hailed me
Through one who evoked you often. Then at last
Your raiser was borne off, and I mourned you had
    passed
    From my life with your late outsetter;
        Till I said, "Tis better!'

But you waylaid me. I rose and went as a ghost goes,
And said, eyes-full: 'I'll never hear it again!
It is overmuch for scathed and memoried men
     When sitting among strange people
          Under their steeple.'

Now, a new stirrer of tones calls you up before me
And wakes your speech, as she of Endor did
(When sought by Saul who, in diguises hid,
     Fell down on the earth to hear it)
          Samuel's spirit.

So, your quired oracles beat till they make me tremble
As I discern your mien in the old attire,
Here in these turmoiled years of belligerent fire
     Living still on – and onward, maybe,
          Till Doom's great day be!

SUNDAY, 13 AUGUST 1916

A HURRIED MEETING

It is August moonlight in the tall plantation,
Whose elms, by aged squirrels' footsteps worn,
   Outscreen the noon, and eve, and morn.
On the facing slope a faint irradiation
   From a mansion's marble front is borne,
     Mute in its woodland wreathing.
   Up here the night-jar whirrs forlorn,
And the trees seem to withhold their softest breathing.

To the moonshade slips a woman in muslin vesture:
Her naked neck the gossamer-web besmears,
   And she sweeps it away with a hasty gesture.
Again it touches her forehead, her neck, her ears,
     Her fingers, the backs of her hands.
     She sweeps it away again
     Impatiently, and then
She takes no notice; and listens, and sighs, and stands.

The night-hawk stops. A man shows in the obscure:
    They meet, and passively kiss,
And he says: 'Well, I've come quickly. About this –
    Is it really so? You are sure?'
  'I am sure. In February it will be.
  That such a thing should come to me!
We should have known. We should have left off
    meeting.
Love is a terrible thing: a sweet allure
    That ends in heart-outeating!'

  'But what shall we do, my Love, and how?'
  'You need not call me by that name now.'
Then he more coldly: 'What is your suggestion?'
  'I've told my mother, and she sees a way,
Since of our marriage there can be no question.
We are crossing South – near about New Year's Day
    The event will happen there.
It is the only thing that we can dare
    To keep them unaware!'
    'Well, you can marry me.'
She shook her head. 'No: that can never be.

"Twill be brought home as hers. She's forty-one,
When many a woman's bearing is not done,
    And well might have a son. –
We should have left off specious self-deceiving:
    I feared that such might come,
    And knowledge struck me numb.
Love is a terrible thing: witching when first begun,
    To end in grieving, grieving!'

And with one kiss again the couple parted:
Inferior clearly he; she haughty-hearted.
He watched her down the slope to return to her place,
The marble mansion of her ancient race,
And saw her brush the gossamers from her face
As she emerged from shade to the moonlight ray.
    And when she had gone away
  The night-jar seemed to imp, and say,
    'You should have taken warning:
Love is a terrible thing: sweet for a space,
    And then all mourning, mourning!'

AFTER A ROMANTIC DAY

The railway bore him through
An earthen cutting out from a city:
    There was no scope for view,
Though the frail light shed by a slim young moon
    Fell like a friendly tune.

    Fell like a liquid ditty,
And the blank lack of any charm
    Of landscape did no harm.
The bald steep cutting, rigid, rough,
    And moon-lit, was enough

For poetry of place: its weathered face
Formed a convenient sheet whereon
The visions of his mind were drawn.

A LAST JOURNEY

   'Father, you seem to have been sleeping fair?'
The child uncovered the dimity-curtained
    window-square
      And looked out at the dawn,
      And back at the dying man nigh gone,
      And propped up in his chair,
Whose breathing a robin's 'chink' took up in antiphon.

      The open fireplace spread
  Like a vast weary yawn above his head,
Its thin blue blower waved
    against his whitening crown,
      For he could not lie down:
He raised him on his arms so emaciated:–

   'Yes; I've slept long, my child. But as for rest,
    Well, that I cannot say.
The whole night have I footed field and turnpike-way –
  A regular pilgrimage – as at my best
    And very briskest day!

"'Twas first to Weatherb'ry, to see them there,
　　　And thence to King's-Stag, where
I joined in a jolly trip to Weydon-Priors Fair:
　　I shot for nuts, bought gingerbreads, cream-cheese;
　　　And, not content with these,
I went to London: heard the watchmen cry the hours.

'I soon was off again, and found me in the bowers
　　　Of father's apple-trees,
　　And he shook the apples down: they fell in showers,
Whereon he turned, smiled strange at me, as ill at ease;
　　And then you pulled the curtain; and, ah me,
　　I found me back where I wished not to be!'

'Twas told the child next day: 'Your father's dead.'
　　　And, struck, she questioned, 'O,
　　That journey, then, did father really go? –
Buy nuts, and cakes, and travel at night
　　　till dawn was red,
　　And tire himself with journeying, as he said,
　　To see those old friends that he cared for so?'

SQUIRE HOOPER

Hooper was ninety. One September dawn
        He sent a messenger
For his physician, who asked thereupon
        What ailed the sufferer
Which he might circumvent, and promptly bid begone.

'Doctor, I summoned you,' the squire replied –
        'Pooh-pooh me though you may –
To ask what's happened to me – burst inside,
        It seems – not much, I'd say –
But awkward with a house-full here for a shoot to-day.'

And he described the symptoms. With bent head
        The listener looked grave.
'H'm ... *You're a dead man in six hours*,' he said. –
        'I speak out, since you are brave –
And best 'tis you should know,
        that last things may be sped.'

'Right,' said the squire. 'And now comes – what to do?
        One thing: on no account
Must I now spoil the sport I've asked them to –
        My guests are paramount –
They must scour scrub and stubble;
        and big bags bring as due.'

He downed to breakfast, and bespoke his guests:—
    'I find I have to go
An unexpected journey, and it rests
    With you, my friends, to show
The shoot can go off gaily, whether I'm there or no.'

Thus blandly spoke he; and to the fields they went,
    And Hooper up the stair.
They had a glorious day; and stiff and spent
    Returned as dusk drew near. —
'Gentlemen,' said the doctor, 'he's not back as meant,

To his deep regret!' — So they took leave, each guest
    Observing: 'I dare say
Business detains him in the town: 'tis best
    We should no longer stay
Just now. We'll come again anon;'
    and they went their way.

Meeting two men in the obscurity
    Shouldering a box a thin
Cloth-covering wrapt, one sportsman cried:
    'Damn me,
    I thought them carrying in,
At first, a coffin; till I knew it could not be.'

IN A WAITING-ROOM

On a morning sick as the day of doom
    With the drizzling gray
    Of an English May,
There were few in the railway waiting-room.
About its walls were framed and varnished
Pictures of liners, fly-blown, tarnished.
The table bore a Testament
For travellers' reading, if suchwise bent.

    I read it on and on,
And, thronging the Gospel of Saint John,
Were figures – additions, multiplications –
    By some one scrawled, with sundry
        emendations;
    Not scoffingly designed,
    But with an absent mind, –
Plainly a bagman's counts of cost,
What he had profited, what lost;
And whilst I wondered if there could have been
    Any particle of a soul
    In that poor man at all,
    To cypher rates of wage
    Upon that printed page,
    There joined in the charmless scene

And stood over me and the scribbled book
    (To lend the hour's mean hue
    A smear of tragedy too)
A soldier and wife, with haggard look
Subdued to stone by strong endeavour;
    And then I heard
    From a casual word
They were parting as they believed for ever.

    But next there came
    Like the eastern flame
Of some high altar, children – a pair –
Who laughed at the fly-blown pictures there.

'Here are the lovely ships that we,
Mother, are by and by going to see!
When we get there it's 'most sure to be fine,
And the band will play, and the sun will shine!'

It rained on the skylight with a din
As we waited and still no train came in;
But the words of the child in the squalid room
Had spread a glory through the gloom.

FAINTHEART IN A RAILWAY TRAIN

At nine in the morning there passed a church,
At ten there passed me by the sea,
At twelve a town of smoke and smirch,
At two a forest of oak and birch,
    And then, on a platform, she:

A radiant stranger, who saw not me.
I said, 'Get out to her do I dare?'
But I kept my seat in my search for a plea,
And the wheels moved on. O could it but be
    That I had alighted there!

THE HARBOUR BRIDGE

From here, the quay, one looks above to mark
The bridge across the harbour, hanging dark
Against the day's-end sky, fair-green in glow
Over and under the middle archway's bow:
It draws its skeleton where the sun has set,
Yea, clear from cutwater to parapet;
On which mild glow, too, lines of rope and spar
     Trace themselves black as char.

Down here in shade we hear the painters shift
Against the bollards with a drowsy lift,
As moved by the incoming stealthy tide.
High up across the bridge the burghers glide
As cut black-paper portraits hastening on
In conversation none knows what upon:
Their sharp-edged lips move quickly word by word
     To speech that is not heard.

There trails the dreamful girl, who leans and stops,
There presses the practical woman to the shops,
There is a sailor, meeting his wife with a start,
And we, drawn nearer, judge they are keeping apart.
Both pause. She says: 'I've looked for you. I thought
We'd make it up.' Then no words can be caught.
At last: 'Won't you come home?'
   She moves still nigher:
      'Tis comfortable, with a fire.'

'No,' he says gloomily. 'And, anyhow,
I can't give up the other woman now:
You should have talked like that in former days
When I was last home.' They go different ways.
And the west dims, and yellow lamplights shine:
And soon above, like lamps more opaline,
White stars ghost forth, that care not for men's wives,
   Or any other lives.

WEYMOUTH

143

AT THE AQUATIC SPORTS

With their backs to the sea two fiddlers stand
Facing the concourse on the strand,
    And a third man who sings.
The sports proceed; there are crab-catchings;
The people laugh as levity spreads;
Yet these three do not turn their heads
    To see whence the merriment springs.

They cease their music, but even then
They stand as before, do those three men,
    Though pausing, nought to do:
They never face to the seaward view
To enjoy the contests, add their cheer,
So wholly is their being here
    A business they pursue.

THE COUNTRY WEDDING
(A FIDDLER'S STORY)

Little fogs were gathered in every hollow,
But the purple hillocks enjoyed fine weather
As we marched with our fiddles over the heather
– How it comes back! – to their wedding that day.

Our getting there brought our neighbours and all, O!
Till, two and two, the couples stood ready.
And her father said: 'Souls, for God's sake, be steady!'
And we strung up our fiddles, and sounded out 'A'.

The groomsman he stared, and said, 'You must follow!'
But we'd gone to fiddle in front of the party,
(Our feelings as friends being true and hearty)
And fiddle in front we did – all the way.

Yes, from their door by Mill-tail-Shallow,
And up Styles-Lane, and by Front-Street houses,
Where stood maids, bachelors, and spouses,
Who cheered the songs that we knew how to play.

I bowed the treble before her father,
Michael the tenor in front of the lady,
The bass-viol Reub – and right well played he! –
The serpent Jim; ay, to church and back.

I thought the bridegroom was flurried rather,
As we kept up the tune outside the chancel,
While they were swearing things none can cancel
Inside the walls to our drumstick's whack.

'Too gay!' she pleaded. 'Clouds may gather,
And sorrow come.' But she gave in, laughing,
And by supper-time when we'd got to the quaffing
Her fears were forgot, and her smiles weren't slack.

A grand wedding 'twas! And what would follow
We never thought. Or that we should have buried her
On the same day with the man that married her,
A day like the first, half hazy, half clear.

Yes: little fogs were in every hollow,
Though the purple hillocks enjoyed fine weather,
When we went to play 'em to church together,
And carried 'em there in an after year.

A TRAMPWOMAN'S TRAGEDY (182—)

I

From Wynyard's Gap the livelong day,
      The livelong day,
We beat afoot the northward way
    We had travelled times before.
The sun-blaze burning on our backs,
Our shoulders sticking to our packs,
By fosseway, fields, and turnpike tracks
    We skirted sad Sedge-Moor.

II

Full twenty miles we jaunted on,
      We jaunted on, –
My fancy-man, and jeering John,
    And Mother Lee, and I.
And, as the sun drew down to west,
We climbed the toilsome Poldon crest,
And saw, of landskip sights the best,
    The inn that beamed thereby.

III

For months we had padded side by side,
> Ay, side by side
Through the Great Forest, Blackmoor wide,
> And where the Parret ran.
We'd faced the gusts on Mendip ridge,
Had crossed the Yeo unhelped by bridge,
Been stung by every Marshwood midge,
> I and my fancy-man.

IV

Lone inns we loved, my man and I,
> My man and I;
'King's Stag', 'Windwhistle' high and dry,
> 'The Horse' on Hintock Green,
The cosy house at Wynyard's Gap,
'The Hut' for quaffs on Bredy Knap,
And many another wayside tap
> Where folk might sit unseen.

V

Now as we trudged – O deadly day,
      O deadly day! –
I teased my fancy-man in play
      And wanton idleness.
I walked alongside jeering John,
I laid his hand my waist upon;
I would not bend my glances on
      My lover's dark distress.

VI

Thus Polden top at last we won,
      At last we won,
And gained the inn at sink of sun
      Far-famed as 'Marshal's Elm'.
Beneath us figured tor and lea,
From Mendip to the western sea –
I doubt if finer sight there be
      Within this royal realm.

VII

Inside the settle all a-row –
    All four a-row
We sat, I next to John, to show
    That he had wooed and won.
And then he took me on his knee,
And swore it was his turn to be
My favoured mate, and Mother Lee
    Passed to my former one.

VIII

Then in a voice I had never heard,
    I had never heard,
My only Love to me: 'One word,
    My lady, if you please!
Whose is the child you are like to bear? –
His? After all my months o' care?'
God knows 'twas not! But, O despair!
    I nodded – still to tease.

IX

Then up he sprung, and with his knife –
    And with his knife
He let out jeering Johnny's life,
    Yes; there, at set of sun.
The slant ray through the window nigh
Gilded John's blood and glazing eye,
Ere scarcely Mother Lee and I
    Knew that the deed was done.

X

The taverns tell the gloomy tale,
    The gloomy tale,
How that at Ivel-chester jail
    My Love, my sweetheart swung;
Though stained till now by no misdeed
Save one horse ta'en in time o'need;
(Blue Jimmy stole right many a steed
    Ere his last fling he flung.)

XI

Thereaft I walked the world alone,
    Alone, alone!
On his death-day I gave my groan
    And dropt his dead-born child.
'Twas nigh the jail, beneath a tree,
None tending me; for Mother Lee
Had died at Glaston, leaving me
    Unfriended on the wild.

XII

And in the night as I lay weak,
    As I lay weak,
The leaves a-falling on my cheek,
    The red moon low declined –
The ghost of him I'd die to kiss
Rose up and said: 'Ah, tell me this!
Was the child mine, or was it his?
    Speak, that I rest may find!'

XIII

O doubt not but I told him then,
     I told him then,
That I had kept me from all men
     Since we joined lips and swore.
Whereat he smiled, and thinned away
As the wind stirred to call up day . . .
– 'Tis past! And here alone I stray
     Haunting the Western Moor.

APRIL 1902

THE CLOCK-WINDER

It is dark as a cave,
Or a vault in the nave
When the iron door
Is closed, and the floor
Of the church relaid
With trowel and spade.

But the parish-clerk
Cares not for the dark
As he winds in the tower
At a regular hour
The rheumatic clock
Whose dilatory knock
You can hear when praying
At the day's decaying,
Or at any lone while
From a pew in the aisle.

Up, up from the ground
Around and around
In the turret stair
He clambers, to where
The wheelwork is,
With its tick, click, whizz,
Reposefully measuring

Each day to its end
That mortal men spend
In sorrowing and pleasuring.
Nightly thus does he climb
To the trackway of Time.

Him I followed one night
To this place without light,
And, ere I spoke, heard
Him say, word by word,
At the end of his winding,
The darkness unminding: –

'So I wipe out one more,
My Dear, of the sore
Sad days that still be,
Like a drying Dead Sea,
Between you and me!'

Who she was no man knew:
He had long borne him blind
To all womankind;
And was ever one who
Kept his past out of view.

THE ABBEY-MASON

INVENTOR OF THE 'PERPENDICULAR' STYLE
OF GOTHIC ARCHITECTURE
(*With Memories of John Hicks, Architect*)

The new-vamped Abbey shaped apace
In the fourteenth century of grace;

(The church which, at an after date,
Acquired cathedral rank and state.)

Panel and circumscribing wall
Of latest feature, trim and tall,

Rose roundabout the Norman core
In prouder pose than theretofore,

Encasing magically the old
With parpend ashlars manifold.

The trowels rang out, and tracery
Appeared where blanks had used to be.

Men toiled for pleasure more than pay,
And all went smoothly day by day,

Till, in due course, the transept part
Engrossed the master-mason's art.

– Home-coming thence he tossed and turned
Throughout the night till the new sun burned.

'What fearful visions have inspired
These gaingivings?' his wife inquired;

'As if your tools were in your hand
You have hammered, fitted, muttered, planned;

'You have thumped as you were working hard:
I might have found me bruised and scarred.

'What then's amiss? What eating care
Looms nigh, whereof I am unaware?'

He answered not, but churchyard went,
Viewing his draughts with discontent;

And fumbled there the livelong day
Till, hollow-eyed, he came away.

– 'Twas said, 'The master-mason's ill!'
And all the abbey works stood still.

Quoth Abbot Wygmore: 'Why, O why
Distress yourself? You'll surely die!'

The mason answered, trouble-torn,
'This long-vogued style is quite outworn!

'The upper archmould nohow serves
To meet the lower tracery curves:

'The ogees bend too far away
To give the flexures interplay.

'This it is causes my distress . . .
So it will ever be unless

'New forms be found to supersede
The circle when occasions need.

'To carry it out I have tried and toiled,
And now perforce must own me foiled!

'Jeerers will say: "Here was a man
Who could not end what he began!" '

– So passed that day, the next, the next;
The abbot scanned the task, perplexed;

The townsmen mustered all their wit
To fathom how to compass it,

But no raw artistries availed
Where practice in the craft had failed . . .

– One night he tossed, all open-eyed,
And early left his helpmeet's side.

Scattering the rushes of the floor
He wandered from the chamber door

And sought the sizing pile, whereon
Struck dimly a cadaverous dawn

Through freezing rain, that drenched the board
Of diagram-lines he last had scored –

Chalked phantasies in vain begot
To knife the architectural knot –

In front of which he dully stood,
Regarding them in hopeless mood.

He closelier looked; then looked again:
The chalk-scratched draught-board faced the rain,

Whose icicled drops deformed the lines
Innumerous of his lame designs,

So that they streamed in small white threads
From the upper segments to the heads

Of arcs below, uniting them
Each by a stalactitic stem.

– At once, with eyes that struck out sparks,
He adds accessory cusping-marks,

Then laughs aloud. The thing was done
So long assayed from sun to sun . . .

– Now in his joy he grew aware
Of one behind him standing there,

And, turning, saw the abbot, who
The weather's whim was watching too.

Onward to Prime the abbot went,
Tacit upon the incident.

– Men now discerned as days revolved
The ogive riddle had been solved;

Templates were cut, fresh lines were chalked
Where lines had been defaced and balked,

And the work swelled and mounted higher,
Achievement distancing desire;

Here jambs with transoms fixed between,
Where never the like before had been –

There little mullions thinly sawn
Where meeting circles once were drawn.

'We knew,' men said, 'the thing would go
After his craft-wit got aglow,

'And, once fulfilled what he has designed,
We'll honour him and his great mind!'

When matters stood thus poised awhile,
And all surroundings shed a smile,

The master-mason on an eve
Homed to his wife and seemed to grieve . . .

– 'The abbot spoke to me to-day;
He hangs about the works alway.

'He knows the source as well as I
Of the new style men magnify.

'He said: "You pride yourself too much
On your creation. Is it such?

' "Surely the hand of God it is
That conjured so, and only His! —

' "Disclosing by the frost and rain
Forms your invention chased in vain;

' "Hence the devices deemed so great
You copied, and did not create."

'I feel the abbot's words are just,
And that all thanks renounce I must.

'Can a man welcome praise and pelf
For hatching art that hatched itself? ...

'So, I shall own the deft design
Is Heaven's outshaping, and not mine.'

'What!' said she. 'Praise your works ensure
To throw away, and quite obscure

'Your beaming and beneficent star?
Better you leave things as they are!

'Why, think awhile. Had not your zest
In your loved craft curtailed your rest –

'Had you not gone there ere the day
The sun had melted all away!'

– But, though his good wife argued so,
The mason let the people know

That not unaided sprang the thought
Whereby the glorious fane was wrought,

But that by frost when dawn was dim
The method was disclosed to him.

'Yet,' said the townspeople thereat,
''Tis your own doing, even with that!'

But he – chafed, childlike, in extremes –
The temperament of men of dreams –

Aloofly scrupled to admit
That he did aught but borrow it,

And diffidently made request
That with the abbot all should rest.

— As none could doubt the abbot's word,
Or question what the church averred,

The mason was at length believed
Of no more count than he conceived,

And soon began to lose the fame
That late had gathered round his name . . .

— Time passed, and like a living thing
The pile went on embodying,

And workmen died, and young ones grew,
And the old mason sank from view

And Abbotts Wygmore and Staunton went
And Horton sped the embellishment.

But not till years had far progressed
Chanced it that, one day, much impressed,

Standing within the well-graced aisle,
He asked who first conceived the style;

And some decrepit sage detailed
How, when invention nought availed,

The cloud-cast waters in their whim
Came down, and gave the hint to him

Who struck each arc, and made each mould;
And how the abbot would not hold

As sole begetter him who applied
Forms the Almighty sent as guide;

And how the master lost renown,
And wore in death no artist's crown.

– Then Horton, who in inner thought
Had more perceptions than he taught,

Replied: 'Nay; art can but transmute;
Invention is not absolute;

'Things fail to spring from nought at call,
And art-beginnings most of all.

'He did but what all artists do,
Wait upon Nature for his cue.'

– 'Had you been here to tell them so,
Lord Abbot, sixty years ago,

'The mason, now long underground,
Doubtless a different fate had found.

'He passed into oblivion dim,
And none knew what became of him!

'His name? 'Twas of some common kind
And now has faded out of mind.'

The Abbott: 'It shall not be hid!
I'll trace it.' ... But he never did.

– When longer yet dank death had wormed
The brain wherein the style had germed

From Gloucester church it flew afar –
The style called Perpendicular. –

To Winton and to Westminster
It ranged, and grew still beautifuller:

From Solway Frith to Dover Strand
Its fascinations starred the land,

Not only on cathedral walls
But upon courts and castle halls,

Till every edifice in the isle
Was patterned to no other style,

And till, long having played its part
The curtain fell on Gothic art.

– Well: when in Wessex on your rounds,
Take a brief step beyond its bounds,

And enter Gloucester: seek the quoin
Where choir and transept interjoin,

And, gazing at the forms there flung
Against the sky by one unsung –

The ogee arches transom-topped,
The tracery-stalks by spandrels stopped,

Petrified lacework – lightly lined
On ancient massiveness behind –

Muse that some minds so modest be
As to renounce fame's fairest fee,

(Like him who crystallized on this spot
His visionings, but lies forgot,

And many a mediaeval one
Whose symmetries salute the sun)

While others boom a baseless claim,
And upon nothing rear a name.

DRAWING DETAILS IN AN
OLD CHURCH

I hear the bell-rope sawing,
And the oil-less axle grind,
As I sit alone here drawing,
What some Gothic brain designed;
And I catch the toll that follows
    From the lagging bell,
Ere it spreads to hills and hollows
    Where people dwell.

I ask not whom it tolls for,
Incurious who he be;
So, some morrow, when those knolls for
One unguessed, sound out for me,
A stranger, loitering under
    In nave or choir,
May think, too, 'Whose, I wonder?'
    But not inquire.

THE OLD WORKMAN

'Why are you so bent down before your time,
Old mason? Many have not left their prime
So far behind at your age, and can still
      Stand full upright at will.'

He pointed to the mansion-front hard by,
And to the stones of the quoin against the sky;
'Those upper blocks,' he said, 'that there you see,
      It was that ruined me.'

There stood in the air up to the parapet
Crowning the corner height, the stones as set
By him – ashlar wheron the gales might drum
      For centuries to come.

'I carried them up,' he said, 'by a ladder there;
The last was as big a load as I could bear,
But on I heaved; and something in my back
      Moved, as 'twere with a crack.

'So I got crookt. I never lost that sprain;
And those who live there, walled from wind and rain
By freestone that I lifted, do not know
      That my life's ache came so.

'They don't know me, or even know my name,
But good I think it, somehow, all the same
To have kept 'em safe from harm, and right and tight,
        Though it has broke me quite.

'Yes; that I fixed it firm up there I am proud,
Facing the hail and snow and sun and cloud,
And to stand storms for ages, beating round
        When I lie underground.'

VETERIS VESTIGIA
FLAMMAE

SHE OPENED THE DOOR

She opened the door of the West to me,
    With its loud sea-lashings,
    And cliff-side clashings
Of waters rife with revelry.

She opened the door of Romance to me,
    The door from a cell
    I had known too well,
Too long, till then, and was fain to flee.

She opened the door of a Love to me,
    That passed the wry
    World-welters by
As far as the arching blue the lea.

She opens the door of the Past to me,
    Its magic lights,
    Its heavenly heights,
When forward little is to see!

1913

THOUGHTS OF PHENA

AT NEWS OF HER DEATH

Not a line of her writing have I,
      Not a thread of her hair,
No mark of her late time as dame in her dwelling,
    whereby
        I may picture her there;
      And in vain do I urge my unsight
        To conceive my lost prize
At her close, whom I knew when her dreams
    were upbrimming with light,
        And with laughter her eyes.

      What scenes spread around her last days,
        Sad, shining, or dim?
Did her gifts and compassions enray
    and enarch her sweet ways
        With an aureate nimb?
      Or did life-light decline from her years,
        And mischances control
Her full day-star; unease, or regret, or forebodings,
    or fears
        Dissenoble her soul?

Thus I do but the phantom retain
       Of the maiden of yore
As my relic; yet haply the best of her –
       fined in my brain
          It may be the more
       That no line of her writing have I,
          Nor a thread of her hair,
No mark of her late time as dame in her dwelling,
       whereby
          I may picture her there.

MARCH 1890

TO LIZBIE BROWNE

I
Dear Lizbie Browne,
Where are you now?
In sun, in rain? –
Or is your brow
Past joy, past pain,
Dear Lizbie Browne?

II
Sweet Lizbie Browne,
How you could smile,
How you could sing! –
How archly wile
In glance-giving,
Sweet Lizbie Browne!

III
And, Lizbie Browne,
Who else had hair
Bay-red as yours,
Or flesh so fair
Bred out of doors,
Sweet Lizbie Browne?

IV

When, Lizbie Browne,
You had just begun
To be endeared
By stealth to one,
You disappeared
My Lizbie Browne!

V

Ay, Lizbie Browne,
So swift your life,
And mine so slow,
You were a wife
Ere I could show
Love, Lizbie Browne.

VI

Still, Lizbie Browne,
You won, they said,
The best of men
When you were wed ...
Where went you then,
O Lizbie Browne?

VII

Dear Lizbie Browne,
I should have thought,
'Girls ripen fast,'
And coaxed and caught
You ere you passed,
Dear Lizbie Browne!

VIII

But, Lizbie Browne,
I let you slip;
Shaped not a sign;
Touched never your lip
With lip of mine,
Lost Lizbie Browne!

IX

So, Lizbie Browne,
When on a day
Men speak of me
As not, you'll say,
'And who was he?' –
Yes, Lizbie Browne!

THE GLIMPSE

She sped through the door
And, following in haste,
And stirred to the core,
I entered hot-faced;
But I could not find her,
No sign was behind her.
'Where is she?' I said:
– 'Who?' they asked that sat there;
'Not a soul's come in sight.'
– 'A maid with red hair.'
– 'Ah.' They paled. 'She is dead.
People see her at night,
But you are the first
On whom she has burst
In the keen common light.'

It was ages ago,
When I was quite strong:
I have waited since, – O,
I have waited so long!
– Yea, I set me to own
The house, where now lone
I dwell in void rooms
Booming hollow as tombs!
But I never come near her,
Though nightly I hear her.
And my cheek has grown thin
And my hair has grown gray
With this waiting therein;
But she still keeps away!

THE OLD GOWN

I have seen her in gowns the brightest,
    Of azure, green, and red,
And in the simplest, whitest,
    Muslined from heel to head;
I have watched her walking, riding,
    Shade-flecked by a leafy tree,
Or in fixed thought abiding
    By the foam-fingered sea.

In woodlands I have known her,
    When boughs were mourning loud,
In the rain-reek she has shown her
    Wild-haired and watery-browed.
And once or twice she has cast me
    As she pomped along the street
Court-clad, ere quite she had passed me,
    A glance from her chariot-seat,

But in my memoried passion
    For evermore stands she
In the gown of fading fashion
    She wore that night when we,
Doomed long to part, assembled
    In the snug small room; yea, when
She sang with lips that trembled,
    'Shall I see his face again?'

TO LOUISA IN THE LANE

Meet me again as at that time
　In the hollow of the lane;
I will not pass as in my prime
　I passed at each day's wane.
　　– Ah, I remember!
To do it you will have to see
Anew this sorry scene wherein you have ceased to be!

But I will welcome your aspen form
　As you gaze wondering round
And say with spectral frail alarm,
　'Why am I still here found?
　　– Ah, I remember!
It is through him with blitheful brow
Who did not love me then,
　but loves and draws me now!'

And I shall answer: 'Sweet of eyes,
　Carry me with you, Dear,
To where you donned this spirit-guise;
　It's better there than here!'
　　– Till I remember
Such is a deed you cannot do:
Wait must I, till with flung-off flesh I follow you.

NOBODY COMES

Tree-leaves labour up and down,
    And through them the fainting light
    Succumbs to the crawl of night.
Outside in the road the telegraph wire
    To the town from the darkening land
Intones to travellers like a spectral lyre
    Swept by a spectral hand.

A car comes up, with lamps full-glare,
    That flash upon a tree:
    It has nothing to do with me,
And whangs along in a world of its own,
    Leaving a black air;
And mute by the gate I stand again alone,
    And nobody pulls up there.

9 OCTOBER 1924

THE MONUMENT-MAKER

I chiselled her monument
    To my mind's content,
Took it to the church by night,
When her planet was at its height,
And set it where I had figured the place in the daytime.
        Having niched it there
I stepped back, cheered, and thought its outlines fair,
        And its marbles rare.

Then laughed she over my shoulder as in our Maytime:
    'It spells not me!' she said:
'Tells nothing about my beauty, wit, or gay time
    With all those, quick and dead,
    Of high or lowlihead,
        That hovered near,
Including you, who carve there your devotion;
    But you felt none, my dear!'

And then she vanished. Checkless sprang my emotion
        And forced a tear
At seeing I'd not been truly known by her,
And never prized! – that my memorial here,
     To consecrate her sepulchre,
       Was scorned, almost,
       By her sweet ghost:
Yet I hoped not quite, in her very innermost!

1916

THE MARBLE TABLET

There it stands, though alas, what a little of her
      Shows in its cold white look!
Not her glance, glide, or smile; not a tittle of her
      Voice like the purl of a brook;
      Not her thoughts, that you read like a book.

It may stand for her once in November
      When first she breathed, witless of all;
Or in heavy years she would remember
      When circumstances held her in thrall;
      Or at last, when she answered her call!

Nothing more. The still marble, date-graven,
      Gives all that it can, tersely lined;
That one has at length found the haven
      Which every one other will find;
      With silence on what shone behind.

ST JULIOT: 8 SEPTEMBER 1916

THE FIGURE IN THE SCENE

It pleased her to step in front and sit
    Where the cragged slope was green,
While I stood back that I might pencil it
    With her amid the scene;
      Till it gloomed and rained;
But I kept on, despite the drifting wet
    That fell and stained
My draught, leaving for curious quizzings yet
    The blots engrained.

And thus I drew her there alone,
    Seated amid the gauze
Of moisture, hooded, only her outline shown,
    With rainfall marked across.
    – Soon passed our stay;
Yet her rainy form is the Genius still of the spot,
    Immutable, yea,
Though the place now knows her no more,
   and has known her not
    Ever since that day.

FROM AN OLD NOTE

ON A MIDSUMMER EVE

I idly cut a parsley stalk,
And blew therein towards the moon;
I had not thought what ghosts would walk
With shivering footsteps to my tune.

I went, and knelt, and scooped my hand
As if to drink, into the brook,
And a faint figure seemed to stand
Above me, with the bygone look.

I lipped rough rhymes of chance, not choice,
I thought not what my words might be;
There came into my ear a voice
That turned a tenderer verse for me.

ON A HEATH

I could hear a gown-skirt rustling
    Before I could see her shape,
Rustling through the heather
    That wove the common's drape,
On that evening of dark weather
    When I hearkened, lips agape.

And when the town-shine in the distance
    Did but baffle here the sight,
And then a voice flew forward:
    'Dear, is't you? I fear the night!'
And the herons flapped to norward
    In the firs upon my right.

There was another looming
    Whose life we did not see;
There was one stilly blooming
    Full nigh to where walked we;
There was a shade entombing
    All that was bright of me.

A COUNTENANCE

Her laugh was not in the middle of her face quite,
    As a gay laugh springs,
It was plain she was anxious about some things
    I could not trace quite.
Her curls were like fir-cones – piled up, brown –
    Or rather like tight-tied sheaves:
It seemed they could never be taken down ...

And her lips were too full, some might say:
I did not think so. Anyway,
The shadow her lower one would cast
Was green in hue whenever she passed
    Bright sun on midsummer leaves.
Alas, I knew not much of her,
And lost all sight and touch of her!

If otherwise, should I have minded
The shy laugh not in the middle of her mouth quite,
And would my kisses have died of drouth quite
    As love became unblinded?

1884

FETCHING HER

An hour before the dawn,
        My friend,
You lit your waiting bedside-lamp
    Your breakfast-fire anon,
And outing into the dark and damp
    You saddled, and set on.

Thuswise, before the day,
        My friend,
You sought her on her surfy shore,
    To fetch her thence away
Unto your own new-builded door
    For a staunch lifelong stay.

You said: 'It seems to be,
        My friend,
That I were bringing to my place
    The pure brine breeze, the sea,
The mews – all her old sky and space,
    In bringing her with me!'

– But time is prompt to expugn,
           My friend,
Such magic-minted conjurings:
   The brought breeze fainted soon,
And then the sense of seamews' wings,
   And the shore's sibilant tune.

   So, it had been more due,
           My friend,
Perhaps, had you not pulled this flower
   From the craggy nook it knew,
And set it in an alien bower;
   But left it where it grew!

AT THE WORD 'FAREWELL'

She looked like a bird from a cloud
    On the clammy lawn,
Moving alone, bare-browed
    In the dim of dawn.
The candles alight in the room
    For my parting meal
Made all things withoutdoors loom
    Strange, ghostly, unreal.

The hour itself was a ghost,
    And it seemed to me then
As of chances the chance furthermost
    I should see her again.
I beheld not where all was so fleet
    That a Plan of the past
Which had ruled us from birthtime to meet
    Was in working at last:

No prelude did I there perceive
     To a drama at all,
Or foreshadow what fortune might weave
     From beginnings so small;
But I rose as if quicked by a spur
     I was bound to obey,
And stepped through the casement to her
     Still alone in the gray.

'I am leaving you ... Farewell!' I said,
     As I followed her on
By an alley bare boughs overspread;
     'I soon must be gone!'
Even then the scale might have been turned
     Against love by a feather,
– But crimson one cheek of hers burned
     When we came in together.

THE LAST PERFORMANCE

'I am playing my oldest tunes,' declared she,
     'All the old tunes I know, –
Those I learnt ever so long ago.'
– Why she should think just then she'd play them
     Silence cloaks like snow.

When I returned from the town at nightfall
     Notes continued to pour
As when I had left two hours before:
'It's the very last time,' she said in closing;
     From now I play no more.'

A few morns onward found her fading,
     And, as her life outflew,
I thought of her playing her tunes right through;
And I felt she had known of what was coming,
     And wondered how she knew.

1912

THE GOING

Why did you give no hint that night
That quickly after the morrow's dawn,
And calmly, as if indifferent quite,
You would close your term here, up and be gone
   Where I could not follow
   With wing of swallow
To gain one glimpse of you ever anon!

   Never to bid good-bye,
   Or lip me the softest call,
Or utter a wish for a word, while I
Saw morning harden upon the wall,
   Unmoved, unknowing
   That your great going
Had place that moment, and altered all.

Why do you make me leave the house
And think for a breath it is you I see
At the end of the alley of bending boughs
Where so often at dusk you used to be;
   Till in darkening dankness
   The yawning blankness
Of the perspective sickens me!

You were she who abode
        By those red-veined rocks far West,
You were the swan-necked one who rode
Along the beetling Beeny Crest,
        And, reining nigh me,
        Would muse and eye me,
While Life unrolled us its very best.

Why, then, latterly did we not speak,
Did we not think of those days long dead,
And ere your vanishing strive to seek
That time's renewal? We might have said,
        'In this bright spring weather
        We'll visit together
Those places that once we visited.'

        Well, well! All's past amend,
            Unchangeable. It must go.
I seem but a dead man held on end
To sink down soon ... O you could not know
        That such swift fleeing
        No soul foreseeing –
Not even I – would undo me so!

DECEMBER 1912

200

YOUR LAST DRIVE

Here by the moorway you returned,
And saw the borough lights ahead
That lit your face – all undiscerned
To be in a week the face of the dead,
And you told of the charm of that haloed view
That never again would beam on you.

And on your left you passed the spot
Where eight days later you were to lie,
And be spoken of as one who was not;
Beholding it with a heedless eye
As alien from you, though under its tree
You soon would halt everlastingly.

I drove not with you ... Yet had I sat
At your side that eve I should not have seen
That the countenance I was glancing at
Had a last-time look at the flickering sheen,
Nor have read the writing upon your face,
'I go hence soon to my resting-place;

'You may miss me then. But I shall not know
How many times you visit me there,
Or what your thoughts are, or if you go
There never at all. And I shall not care.
Should you censure me I shall take no heed,
And even your praises no more shall need.'

True: never you'll know. And you will not mind.
But shall I then slight you because of such?
Dear ghost, in the past did you ever find
The thought 'What profit,' move me much?
Yet abides the fact, indeed, the same, –
You are past love, praise, indifference, blame.

DECEMBER 1912

THE WALK

You did not walk with me
Of late to the hill-top tree
      By the gated ways,
      As in earlier days;
      You were weak and lame,
      So you never came,
And I went alone, and I did not mind,
Not thinking of you as left behind.

      I walked up there to-day
      Just in the former way;
        Surveyed around
        The familiar ground
        By myself again:
        What difference, then?
Only that underlying sense
Of the look of a room on returning thence.

RAIN ON A GRAVE

Clouds spout upon her
        Their waters amain
        In ruthless disdain, –
Her who but lately
        Had shivered with pain
As at touch of dishonour
If there had lit on her
So coldly, so straightly
        Such arrows of rain:

One who to shelter
        Her delicate head
Would quicken and quicken
        Each tentative tread
If drops chanced to pelt her
        That summertime spills
        In dust-paven rills
When thunder-clouds thicken
        And birds close their bills.

Would that I lay there
    And she were housed here!
Or better, together
Were folded away there
Exposed to one weather
We both, – who would stray there
When sunny the day there,
    Or evening was clear
    At the prime of the year.

Soon will be growing
    Green blades from her mound,
And daisies be showing
    Like stars on the ground,
Till she form part of them –
Ay – the sweet heart of them,
    Loved beyond measure
    With a child's pleasure
    All her life's round.

31 JANUARY, 1913

I FOUND HER OUT THERE

I found her out there
On a slope few see,
That falls westwardly
To the salt-edged air,
Where the ocean breaks
On the purple strand,
And the hurricane shakes
The solid land.

I brought her here,
And have laid her to rest
In a noiseless nest
No sea beats near.
She will never be stirred
In her loamy cell
By the waves long heard
And loved so well.

So she does not sleep
By those haunted heights
The Atlantic smites
And the blind gales sweep,
Whence she often would gaze
At Dundagel's famed head,
While the dipping blaze
Dyed her face fire-red;

And would sigh at the tale
Of sunk Lyonnesse,
As a wind-tugged tress
Flapped her cheek like a flail:
Or listen at whiles
With a thought-bound brow
To the murmuring miles
She is far from now.

Yet her shade, maybe,
Will creep underground
Till it catch the sound
Of that western sea
As it swells and sobs
Whence she once domiciled,
And joy in its throbs
With the heart of a child.

WITHOUT CEREMONY

It was your way, my dear,
To vanish without a word
When callers, friends, or kin
Had left, and I hastened in
To rejoin you, as I inferred.

And when you'd a mind to career
Off anywhere – say to town –
You were all on a sudden gone
Before I had thought thereon,
Or noticed your trunks were down.

So, now that you disappear
For ever in that swift style,
Your meaning seems to me
Just as it used to be:
'Good-bye is not worth while!'

LAMENT

How she would have loved
A party to-day! –
Bright-hatted and gloved,
With table and tray
And chairs on the lawn
Her smiles would have shone
With welcomings . . . But
She is shut, she is shut
⠀⠀⠀From friendship's spell
⠀⠀⠀In the jailing shell
⠀⠀⠀Of her tiny cell.

Or she would have reigned
At a dinner to-night
With ardours unfeigned,
And a generous delight;
All in her abode
She'd have freely bestowed
On her guests . . . But alas,
She is shut under grass
⠀⠀⠀Where no cups flow,
⠀⠀⠀Powerless to know
⠀⠀⠀That it might be so.

And she would have sought
With a child's eager glance
The shy snowdrops brought
By the new year's advance,
And peered in the rime
Of Candlemas-time
For crocuses ... chanced
It that she were not tranced
From sights she loved best;
Wholly possessed
By an infinite rest!

And we are here staying
Amid these stale things,
Who care not for gaying,
And those junketings
That used so to joy her,
And never to cloy her
As us they cloy! ... But
She is shut, she is shut
From the cheer of them, dead
To all done and said
In her yew-arched bed.

THE HAUNTER

He does not think that I haunt here nightly:
    How shall I let him know
That whither his fancy sets him wandering
    I, too, alertly go? –
Hover and hover a few feet from him
    Just as I used to do,
But cannot answer the words he lifts me –
    Only listen thereto!

When I could answer he did not say them:
    When I could let him know
How I would like to join in his journeys
    Seldom he wished to go.
Now that he goes and wants me with him
    More than he used to do,
Never he sees my faithful phantom
    Though he speaks thereto.

Yes, I companion him to places
     Only dreamers know,
Where the shy hares print long paces,
     Where the night rooks go;
Into old aisles where the past is all to him,
     Close as his shade can do,
Always lacking the power to call to him,
     Near as I reach thereto!

What a good haunter I am, O tell him!
     Quickly make him know
If he but sigh since my loss befell him
     Straight to his side I go.
Tell him a faithful one is doing
     All that love can do
Still that his path may be worth pursuing,
     And to bring peace thereto.

THE VOICE

Woman much missed, how you call to me, call to me,
Saying that now you are not as you were
When you had changed
    from the one who was all to me,
But as at first, when our day was fair.

Can it be you that I hear? Let me view you, then,
Standing as when I drew near to the town
Where you would wait for me: yes, as I knew you then,
Even to the original air-blue gown!

Or is it only the breeze, in its listlessness
Travelling across the wet mead to me here,
You being ever dissolved to wan wistlessness,
Heard no more again far or near?

    Thus I; faltering forward,
    Leaves around me falling,
Wind oozing thin through the thorn from norward,
    And the woman calling.

DECEMBER 1912

HIS VISITOR

I come across from Mellstock
    while the moon wastes weaker
To behold where I lived with you
    for twenty years and more:
I shall go in the gray, at the passing of the mail-train,
And need no setting open of the long familiar door
        As before.

The change I notice in my once own quarters!
A formal-fashioned border where the daisies used to
    be,
The rooms new painted, and the pictures altered,
And other cups and saucers, and no cosy nook for tea
        As with me.

I discern the dim faces of the sleep-wrapt servants;
They are not those who tended me through feeble
      hours and strong,
But strangers quite, who never knew my rule here,
Who never saw me painting,
        never heard my softling song
             Float along.

So I don't want to linger in this re-decked dwelling,
I feel too uneasy at the contrasts I behold,
And I make again for Mellstock to return here never,
And rejoin the roomy silence,
        and the mute and manifold
            Souls of old.

1913

A DREAM OR NO

Why go to Saint-Juliot? What's Juliot to me?
                    Some strange necromancy
                    But charmed me to fancy
That much of my life claims the spot as its key.

Yes. I have had dreams of that place in the West,
                    And a maiden abiding
                    Thereat as in hiding;
Fair-eyed and white-shouldered,
        broad-browed and brown-tressed.

And of how, coastward bound on a night long ago,
                    There lonely I found her,
                    The sea-birds around her,
And other than nigh things uncaring to know.

So sweet her life there (in my thought has it seemed)
                    That quickly she drew me
                    To take her unto me,
And lodge her long years with me.
        Such have I dreamed.

But nought of that maid from Saint-Juliot I see;
　　　　Can she ever have been here,
　　　　And shed her life's sheen here,
The woman I thought a long housemate with me?

Does there even a place like Saint-Juliot exist?
　　　　Or a Vallency Valley
　　　　With stream and leafed alley,
Or Beeny, or Bos with its flounce flinging mist?

FEBRUARY 1913

AFTER A JOURNEY

Hereto I come to view a voiceless ghost;
 Whither, O whither will its whim now draw me?
Up the cliff, down, till I'm lonely, lost,
 And the unseen waters' ejaculations awe me.
Where you will next be there's no knowing,
 Facing round about me everywhere,
  With your nut-coloured hair,
And gray eyes, and rose-flush coming and going.

Yes: I have re-entered your olden haunts at last;
 Through the years, through the dead scenes I
  have tracked you;
What have you now found to say of our past –
 Scanned across the dark space wherein
  I have lacked you?
Summer gave us sweets,
  but autumn wrought division?
 Things were not lastly as firstly well
  With us twain, you tell?
But all's closed now, despite Time's derision.

I see what you are doing: you are leading me on
      To the spots we knew
          when we haunted here together,
The waterfall, above which the mist-bow shone
      At the then fair hour in the then fair weather,
And the cave just under, with a voice still so hollow
      That it seems to call out to me
          from forty years ago,
              When you were all aglow,
And not the thin ghost that I now frailly follow!

Ignorant of what there is flitting here to see,
      The waked birds preen and the seals flop lazily;
Soon you will have, Dear, to vanish from me,
      For the stars close their shutters
          and the dawn whitens hazily.
Trust me, I mind not, though Life lours,
      The bringing me here; nay, bring me here again!
          I am just the same as when
Our days were a joy, and our paths through flowers.

PENTARGAN BAY

BEENY CLIFF
MARCH 1870–MARCH 1913

I

O the opal and the sapphire
    of that wandering western sea,
And the woman riding high above
    with bright hair flapping free –
The woman whom I loved so,
    and who loyally loved me.

II

The pale mews plained below us,
    and the waves seemed far away
In a nether sky, engrossed in saying
    their ceaseless babbling say,
As we laughed light-heartedly aloft
    on that clear-sunned March day.

III

A little cloud then cloaked us,
    and there flew an irised rain,
And the Atlantic dyed its levels
    with a dull misfeatured stain,
And then the sun burst out again,
    and purples prinked the main.

IV

– Still in all its chasmal beauty bulks
    old Beeny to the sky,
And shall she and I not go there
    once again now March is nigh
And the sweet things said in that March
    say anew there by and by?

What if still in chasmal beauty looms
    that wild weird western shore,
The woman now is – elsewhere –
    whom the ambling pony bore,
And nor knows nor cares for Beeny,
    and will laugh there nevermore.

AT CASTLE BOTEREL

As I drive to the junction of lane and highway,
      And the drizzle bedrenches the waggonette,
I look behind at the fading byway,
      And see on its slope, now glistening wet,
            Distinctly yet

Myself and a girlish form benighted
      In dry March weather. We climb the road
Beside a chaise. We had just alighted
      To ease the sturdy pony's load
            When he sighed and slowed.

What we did as we climbed, and what we talked of
      Matters not much, nor to what it led, –
Something that life will not be balked of
      Without rude reason till hope is dead,
            And feeling fled.

It filled but a minute. But was there ever
      A time of such quality, since or before,
In that hill's story? To one mind never,
      Though it has been climbed, foot-swift, foot-sore,
            By thousands more.

Primaeval rocks form the road's steep border,
    And much have they faced there, first and last,
Of the transitory in Earth's long order;
    But what they record in colour and cast
        Is – that we two passed.

And to me, though Time's unflinching rigour,
    In mindless rote, has ruled from sight
The substance now, one phantom figure
    Remains on the slope, as when that night
        Saw us alight.

I look and see it there, shrinking, shrinking,
    I look back at it amid the rain
For the very last time; for my sand is sinking,
    And I shall traverse old love's domain
        Never again.

MARCH 1913

PLACES

Nobody says: Ah, that is the place
Where chanced, in the hollow of years ago,
What none of the Three Towns cared to know –
The birth of a little girl of grace –
The sweetest the house saw, first or last;
      Yet it was so
      On that day long past.

Nobody thinks: There, there she lay
In a room by the Hoe, like the bud of a flower,
And listened, just after the bedtime hour,
To the stammering chimes that used to play
The quaint Old Hundred-and-Thirteenth tune
      In Saint Andrew's tower
      Night, morn, and noon.

Nobody calls to mind that here
Upon Boterel Hill, where the waggoners skid,
With cheeks whose airy flush outbid
Fresh fruit in bloom, and free of fear,
She cantered down, as if she must fall
      (Though she never did),
      To the charm of all.

Nay: one there is to whom these things,
That nobody else's mind calls back,
Have a savour that scenes in being lack,
And a presence more than the actual brings;
To whom to-day is beneaped and stale,
       And its urgent clack
       But a vapid tale.

PLYMOUTH, MARCH 1913

THE SPELL OF THE ROSE

'I mean to build a hall anon,
        And shape two turrets there,
        And a broad newelled stair,
And a cool well for crystal water;
        Yes; I will build a hall anon,
        Plant roses love shall feed upon,
        And apple-trees and pear.'

He set to build the manor-hall,
        And shaped the turret there,
        And the broad newelled stair,
And the cool well for crystal water;
        He built for me that manor-hall,
        And planted many trees withal,
        But no rose anywhere.

And as he planted never a rose
        That bears the flowers of love,
        Though other flowers throve
Some heart-bane moved our souls to sever
        Since he had planted never a rose;
        And misconceits raised horrid shows,
        And agonies came thereof.

'I'll mend these miseries,' then said I,
　　And so, at dead of night,
　　I went and, screened from sight,
That nought should keep our souls in severance,
　　I set a rose-bush, 'This,' said I,
　　　'May end divisions dire and wry,
　　　And long-drawn days of blight.'

But I was called from earth – yea, called
　　Before my rose-bush grew;
　　And would that now I knew
What feels he of the tree I planted,
　　And whether, after I was called
　　To be a ghost, he, as of old,
　　　Gave me his heart anew!

Perhaps now blooms that queen of trees
　　I set but saw not grow,
　　And he, beside its glow –
Eyes couched of the mis-vision that blurred me –
　　Ay, there beside that queen of trees
　　He sees me as I was, though sees
　　　Too late to tell me so!

ST LAUNCE'S REVISITED

     Slip back, Time!
Yet again I am nearing
Castle and keep, uprearing
     Gray, as in my prime.

     At the inn
Smiling nigh, why is it
Not as on my visit
     When hope and I were twin?

     Groom and jade
Whom I found here, moulder;
Strange the tavern-holder,
     Strange the tap-maid.

     Here I hired
Horse and man for bearing
Me on my wayfaring
     To the door desired.

Evening gloomed
As I journeyed forward
To the faces shoreward,
    Till their dwelling loomed.

If again
Towards the Atlantic sea there
I should speed, they'd be there
    Surely now as then? . . .

Why waste thought,
When I know them vanished
Under earth; yea, banished
    Ever into nought!

WHERE THE PICNIC WAS

Where we made the fire
In the summer time
Of branch and briar
On the hill to the sea,
I slowly climb
Through winter mire,
And scan and trace
The forsaken place
Quite readily.

Now a cold wind blows,
And the grass is gray,
But the spot still shows
As a burnt circle – aye,
And stick-ends, charred,
Still strew the sward
Whereon I stand,
Last relic of the band
Who came that day!

Yes, I am here
Just as last year,
And the sea breathes brine
From its strange straight line
Up hither, the same
As when we four came.

— But two have wandered far
From this grassy rise
Into urban roar
Where no picnics are,
And one — has shut her eyes
For evermore.

AFTERWARDS

DURING WIND AND RAIN

They sing their dearest songs –
He, she, all of them – yea,
Treble and tenor and bass,
    And one to play;
With the candles mooning each face . . .
    Ah, no; the years O!
How the sick leaves reel down in throngs!

They clear the creeping moss –
Elders and juniors – aye,
Making the pathways neat
    And the garden gay;
And they build a shady seat . . .
    Ah, no; the years, the years;
See, the white storm-birds wing across!

They are blithely breakfasting all –
Men and maidens – yea,
Under the summer tree,
    With a glimpse of the bay,
While pet fowl come to the knee . . .
    Ah, no; the years O!
And the rotten rose is ript from the wall.

They change to a high new house,
He, she, all of them – aye,
Clocks and carpets and chairs
    On the lawn all day,
And brightest things that are theirs . . .
    Ah, no; the years, the years;
Down their carved names the rain-drop ploughs.

WE ARE GETTING TO THE END

We are getting to the end of visioning
The impossible within this universe,
Such as that better whiles may follow worse,
And that our race may mend by reasoning.

We know that even as larks in cages sing
Unthoughtful of deliverance from the curse
That holds them lifelong in a latticed hearse,
We ply spasmodically our pleasuring.

And that when nations set them to lay waste
Their neighbours' heritage by foot and horse,
And hack their pleasant plains in festering seams,
They may again, – not warely, or from taste,
But tickled mad by some demonic force. –
Yes. We are getting to the end of dreams!

IN TIME OF 'THE BREAKING OF NATIONS'

I

Only a man harrowing clods
    In a slow silent walk
With an old horse that stumbles and nods
    Half asleep as they stalk.

II

Only thin smoke without flame
    From the heaps of couch-grass;
Yet this will go onward the same
    Though Dynasties pass.

III

Yonder a maid and her wight
    Come whispering by:
War's annals will cloud into night
    Ere their story die.

1915

CHRISTMAS: 1924

'Peace upon earth!' was said. We sing it,
And pay a million priests to bring it.
After two thousand years of mass
We've got as far as poison-gas.

1924

AFTERWARDS

When the Present has latched its postern behind
  my tremulous stay,
 And the May month flaps its glad green leaves
   like wings,
Delicate-filmed as new-spun silk,
  will the neighbours say,
 'He was a man who used to notice such things'?

If it be in the dusk when,
  like an eyelid's soundless blink,
 The dewfall-hawk comes crossing the shades
   to alight
Upon the wind-warped upland thorn,
  a gazer may think,
 'To him this must have been a familiar sight.'

If I pass during some nocturnal blackness,
  mothy and warm,
 When the hedgehog travels furtively over the lawn,
One may say, 'He strove that such innocent creatures
  should come to no harm,
 But he could do little for them; and now he is gone.'

If, when hearing that I have been stilled at last,
    they stand at the door,
  Watching the full-starred heavens that winter sees,
Will this thought rise on those who will meet
    my face no more,
   'He was one who had an eye for such mysteries'?

And will any say when my bell of quittance
    is heard in the gloom,
  And a crossing breeze cuts a pause in its outrollings,
Till they rise again, as they were a new bell's boom,
   'He hears it not now, but used to notice such things'?

WHEN I SET OUT FOR LYONNESSE
(1870)

When I set out for Lyonnesse,
  A hundred miles away,
  The rime was on the spray,
And starlight lit my lonesomeness
When I set out for Lyonnesse
  A hundred miles away.

What would bechance at Lyonnesse
  While I should soujourn there
  No prophet durst declare,
Nor did the wisest wizard guess
What would bechance at Lyonnesse
  While I should soujourn there.

When I came back from Lyonnesse
  With magic in my eyes,
  All marked with mute surmise
My radiance rare and fathomless,
When I came back from Lyonnesse
  With magic in my eyes!

HE NEVER EXPECTED MUCH

[OR] A CONSIDERATION
[*A reflection*] ON MY EIGHTY-SIXTH BIRTHDAY

Well, World, you have kept faith with me,
          Kept faith with me;
Upon the whole you have proved to be
          Much as you said you were.
Since as a child I used to lie
Upon the leaze and watch the sky,
Never, I own, expected I
          That life would all be fair.

'Twas then you said, and since have said,
          Times since have said,
In that mysterious voice you shed
          From clouds and hills around:
'Many have loved me desperately,
Many with smooth serenity,
While some have shown contempt of me
          Till they dropped underground.

'I do not promise overmuch,
      Child; overmuch;
Just neutral-tinted haps and such,'
      You said to minds like mine.
Wise warning for your credit's sake!
Which I for one failed not to take,
And hence could stem such strain and ache
      As each year might assign.

EPITAPH ON A PESSIMIST

I'm Smith of Stoke, aged sixty-odd,
    I've lived without a dame
From youth-time on; and would to God
    My dad had done the same.

FROM THE FRENCH AND GREEK

A POET

Attentive eyes, fantastic heed,
Assessing minds, he does not need,
Nor urgent writs to sup or dine,
Nor pledges in the rosy wine.

For loud acclaim he does not care
By the august or rich or fair,
Nor for smart pilgrims from afar,
Curious on where his hauntings are.

But soon or later, when you hear
That he has doffed this wrinkled gear,
Some evening, at the first star-ray
Come to his graveside, pause and say:

'Whatever his message – glad or grim –
Two bright-souled women clave to him;'
Stand and say that while day decays;
It will be word enough of praise.

JULY 1914

THE WEARY WALKER

A plain in front of me,
    And there's the road
Upon it. Wide country,
    And, too, the road!

Past the first ridge another,
    And still the road
Creeps on. Perhaps no other
    Ridge for the road?

Ah! Past that ridge a third,
    Which still the road
Has to climb furtherward –
    The thin white road!

Sky seems to end its track;
    But no. The road
Trails down the hill at the back.
    Ever the road!

INDEX OF FIRST LINES